TALK LIKE JESUS

CHANGE YOUR WORLD WITH THE S.I.M.P.L.E.™ STEPS OF THE MASTER COMMUNICATOR

LYNN WILFORD SCARBOROUGH

ISBN: 1-59777-559-2
Library of Congress Cataloging-In-Publication Data Available

Book Design by: Sonia Fiore

Printed in the United States of America

Phoenix Books, Inc.
9465 Wilshire Boulevard, Suite 315
Beverly Hills, CA 90212

10 9 8 7 6 5 4 3 2 1

TABLE OF CONTENTS

JESUS
PROFILE OF THE
MASTER COMMUNICATOR

He is called Master by some and a Master Communicator by all. Born in a barn, raised in a ghetto and a common laborer by trade, Jesus spoke in obscurity, yet his message changed the world and continues to be repeated millions of times each day. Majesty aside, what did Jesus of Nazareth do to have such influence?

Jesus changed the paradigms of his world with simple stories. He used older truths to unravel the lies around him. Like a trumpet his words shook the foundations with critical questions like, "Why?"

From many perspectives, his life was a paradox. He owned nothing but was the son of a king. He was simple and direct, but mysterious and unfathomable. Jesus was spiritual, but not religious. He lived in harmony with the law, but was not crushed by it. Jesus lived in total freedom, yet walked in total obedience. He was calm in the midst of storms and unwavering in his purpose.

Like all revolutionaries, Jesus dealt with the challenges of public life. What can we learn from the way he prepared his presentations, mentored his team, established boundaries and stayed on message, even when exhausted and in the face of death?

Jesus' messages were common yet classic, plain yet complex, simple yet revolutionary, childlike yet ageless, ordinary yet multifaceted, familiar yet unforgettable. His messages have been memorized, analyzed, dramatized and computerized. It is undeniable that Jesus' words have power and depths of meaning waiting to be explored.

AUTHOR FOREWORD
Why Should We Talk Like Jesus?

All we desire, love, hope and dream is birthed by words.
All we are is linked to our ability to communicate out and receive in.
All we struggle with, battle for, resist, pushback and stand against grows from our communication abilities, disabilities and disconnects.
Communication is the Alpha and the Omega of our lives.
It is the seed that plants, the key that unlocks, the coin that pays, the light that directs, the vehicle that gets us there, the signal that transmits, the armor that protects and the lock that secures the contract.

Communication – The Universal Key for Success

Communication is one of the most remarkable of humanity's gifts and also the greatest of man's individual fears. All parts of our being – spirit, soul and body – depend on communication to function. Communication is the key to our lives, families, relationships, careers and passions. Without effective communication situations disconnect, opportunities flounder, relationships dissolve and products are forgotten.

All industries, from financial to fashion, from energy to entertainment depend on communication for their marketing and success. Great communicators make great leaders, and excellent communication skills are critical to professional success. To help "get their message out" and to fuel sales and convert images into dollars, the business world spends millions of dollars annually training and equipping their employees with communication tools and skills.

Success does have a formula, and wisdom searches it out. That is why it is imperative to learn from the best. Artists copy the masters, scientists practice the formulas, musicians play the classics and athletes study the winners.

How Do We Master Communication?

We learn by following a master. Learning from his ways. Listening to his words. Seeing the shape of his message. Measuring the weight of his information. Reviewing the images he chose. Watching how he prepared for his battles. Feeling the truth in his resolve.

Jesus' communication was like a brilliant diamond. No matter what direction you looked at it, the light shown through the facets. What added to its brilliance was how simple, direct, clean, and uncluttered his message was. Even when being attacked viciously he was brilliant in his questions and strategic in his answers. He was creative, interesting, focused and exacting in all that he did.

Do Jesus' Communication Techniques Work in a Media Saturated World?

Jesus was a brilliant communicator and extraordinary teacher. This book endeavors to identify and reveal some of his secrets. Like a CAT scan to observe the hidden structures, this book evaluates the presentation style of Jesus of Nazareth with a modern media lens and through the twenty years experience of a professional TV media coach and corporate communications trainer.

Jesus' methods are explored and analyzed to find if they are relevant. Do his techniques have universal application? Will they work in our high tech, high-speed world? The answer is yes, amazingly well.

From this book it is hoped that you may gain insights, principles and specific applications that you may apply to any and every communication situation in your life. Jesus demonstrated that it was possible to use these communication techniques with family, friends, and foes. They can be used in the comfort of a home, a fast-paced management situation or in a public media battlefield.

Talk Like Jesus explores and discusses the techniques and skills of a Master Communicator – Jesus of Nazareth. Here are some specifics that can be learned from this book.

DAILY COMMUNICATION – GET CONNECTED

Jesus' techniques teach us how to connect with people quickly and effectively. Learn how to use stories, analogies, questions and interaction to "hook" and engage in every area – personal, business or ministry.

MESSAGE CONTENT – BE CREATIVE AND MEMORABLE

Jesus' messages were prepared and shaped for maximum and long-term impact. Like the best commercials ever seen, he used stories, word pictures and similes to impact the audience. These principles will help you shape your communication, even when you don't have a lot of time to prepare, so that it is memorable and sticks like Velcro in people's minds.

COMMUNICATION FOCUS – GET RESULTS

These methods and techniques will empower you to communicate with more control, focus, creativity and results. We hope that this will improve your sales, marketing, management techniques, presentations and media interviews as well as chats with your kids. A side benefit is that employing these techniques will also help improve writing skills, emails, press releases and phone discourse.

LESS WORDS – GREATER IMPACT

In a world filled with trillions of words and millions of commercials, what's a person to do? If anyone demonstrated the less is more principle of communication it was Jesus. This book will inspire and teach you how to make information simpler, cleaner and less cluttered. This builds confidence and when you are more relaxed, your audience will enjoy your presentations more, and so will you!

BETTER PREPARED – LESS WORK

Getting ready for a presentation, speech or media interview is much easier when you know how to focus and execute. Jesus' method gives a template to help you prepare for any communication situation.

USING QUESTIONS – BE STRATEGIC

Jesus used questions offensively and defensively. He used them to open and engage people's minds. In aggressive situations he used them like a shield to deflect and protect. The more questions we use, the wiser people think we are, because questions make us smarter, if we listen to the answers.

LESS CONFLICT – LESS GUILT

It is important to recognize the times and reasons Jesus did *not* respond. Jesus established communication boundaries with those who were negative, manipulative or aggressive. This means that you don't have to feel guilty or waste time with toxic individuals, set-ups and no wins. Like Jesus, we can learn when to just say no.

MULTI-CONNECTED – BETTER RESPONSE

Jesus knew that people communicate on many levels and used his images and questions to reach them. A person may ask for a fact, but really need a word of encouragement. Do they need an answer from the heart, head or spirit? The more we can tune into a person's needs and frequencies, the more impact our communication will have.

LESS FEAR – MORE CONFIDENCE AND FREEDOM

We all have been wounded by words and dealt with fear. Jesus' methods will help build confidence and combat fear because they get results. Learning to use these techniques is fun and makes you want to keep trying.

OVERCOME COMMUNICATION DIFFICULTIES – LESS STRESS

We all have difficult communication situations, so did Jesus. Learning from his example helps us deal with communication problems at home, work or when in the media spotlight. While we will never be able to avoid conflict, we can learn how to deal with the situation and the "turkeys" when they land in our office.

FASTER RECONNECTION – LESS WASTED TIME

If the lamp is unplugged, we reconnect it. When communication is unplugged, we have to reconnect also. Learning Jesus' principles will give you skills so you can figure out where and how to fix the disconnects. This book will give you some tools to help you plug back in and "ping" to make sure that communication is back on track.

MORE LAUGHS – BETTER USE OF HUMOR

Professional speakers know that laughter is the fastest way to engage people. From a personal perspective, even though I have always used humor in my presentations, since using Jesus' techniques, my laugh count has increased. This was totally unexpected, but what a benefit! I'm not writing any jokes, but simply telling stories from the heart, honestly. I am confident that like every great storyteller, Jesus had a great sense of humor.

When used with grace, humor is a mirror that lets us see what is right in front of us. Also, humor shines a spotlight on the truth of a person's actions without directly attacking their motives. Humor turns our mistakes into joyful packets of wisdom. When I am free enough to laugh at my errors and weaknesses, it's as if the laughter puts wings on my mistakes; and they fly away to the heavens. Laughter frees me, frees all of me, and frees us all from the chains that bind. Oh how we need to laugh!

MORE SPIRIT – MORE JOY

Like a wonderful breeze through the trees that moves the clouds, communication is the essence of life. Jesus communicated fully, from all parts – spirit, soul and body – and taught others to do the same. Using Jesus' techniques helps people to reconnect with themselves and connect with others. We are fully whole and healed only within community, and that means we have to talk, listen, question, joke and love, encourage and touch continually.

THE MISSION POSSIBLE

Even though it is impossible to separate the mission from the man, it is possible to evaluate the communication methods that Jesus used. This book takes a look at Jesus' communication style with a modern eye. *Talk Like Jesus* has been written to explore the genius and understand the classic principles of communication of Jesus Christ. The evaluation of his methods has resulted in a solid model, principles, how-tos and applications that everyone can use.

There are principles in this book that will be familiar and well known. That is to be expected because like the opening notes of a popular song, truth is like music to our spirits. However, though the tune is familiar, the arrangement is new. The cross-pollination of information has shaped a new communications mural. As the summation of a diverse twenty-year career journey, *Talk Like Jesus* has grown from a variety of professional media environments and reflects these new paradigms. They may not all apply to you or your situation, but, as I tell my clients during coaching sessions: Take the information and principles that you need – leave the rest. In writing this book it has been my desire that these principles be expressed in simplicity twined with clarity. You may judge how well I did, but please be kind.

One of my favorite proverbs states that, "A fool delighteth not in understanding but only expressing their own opinion." In effort not to be considered a fool, this book endeavors to provide understanding and usable information. You will see that each key point is followed by a communication principle and the practical applications of the rule. On information that is more spiritual in nature (discussion of a word or interpretation) or regarding my opinion (questions, spiritual musings or experiences), these have been placed in boxes as sidebars, so that readers may skip or peruse at their own discretion.

My experience and training gives me a unique perspective, and these insights are what I hope is of value. The majority of my life's work has been helping people improve their communication skills. It doesn't matter if you are a TV anchor or a third grader; I love helping people get better. To empower others is an honor, privilege, joy and responsibility.

The primary goal of this book is to help you become **a better communicator**. If that is accomplished then mission accomplished.

The secondary goal of this book is very private. I hope that it makes you think about things that are life-giving. And, as the thoughts come and rejuvenate your spirit, I pray you will be energized enough to take action. May you make time for a tender late night conversation, a giggle with a child, and a walk with a dear friend (human or non) or dial the number of a distant forgotten friend.

Even though there are spiritual reflections contained within the book, I do not consider myself a theologian. I am a follower of Jesus on a very unusual journey.

HERE'S THE KEY

If you were offered the key to a vault of jewels that you could access whenever you wanted, would you take it? When we study Jesus' communication style it is a key to a treasure chest of opportunity. The principles, techniques and methods are waiting to unlock all the brilliance and jewels that rest within you. May the words that follow help you unlock your desires and truth, known and unknown. May this book be a gentle guide in your quest for communication mastery.

Before moving into the nature of our hyper-media world, I want to thank you again for taking the time to join in this discovery. Please remember that this book is the first threshold to an evolving body of communication understanding. I don't have all the answers, but for some, these reflections will be an epiphany; for others, a review; and others still, a launching point to greater heights. What ever it is, I say go for it. Let us know what you find when you get there. Write to me when you find more revelation – we all have lots to learn.

PROFILE
Imagine a Hill

Imagine a hill in Galilee; it is a country setting during New Testament times. The sun is hot, but the persistent breeze from the gentle sea nearby is enough to cool your face. There are people everywhere. Children dash around in loose huddles of five or six. There are women with nursing babies wrapped like cocoons across their shoulders, young men with dirt on their hands, and old men with dirt on their feet.

You have been traveling for several months with the group that is following Yeshua of Nazareth (Jesus). You first heard of this teacher after being baptized in the Jordan by the wild preacher called Joachim (John). You had walked with your brothers for two days into the desert to listen and be baptized by Joachim and then returned home to help with the vineyard. You wanted to travel further down river to listen to this carpenter turned teacher, but you had promised your father to return and help with the harvest.

Then several months later, Yeshua came near your village. You weren't sure why you first went to hear him, except when he spoke his words were like rocks tossed into a bed of coals. Sparks flew up into the night sky and flames danced beyond the fire pit; the words and images of this man stirred and set fire to your heart and mind. The stories stayed inside your head, but they created more questions than they answered. You had only intended to spend one short evening listening to him teach, but then after a sleepless night of questions, you returned the next morning, day, evening and day after that. The very presence of this carpenter caused you to sit as close as possible and linger long after the crowds had left to gather the crumbs of explanations that might drop during the conversations.

Never had you heard such teaching. Like opening a pomegranate for the first time, Yeshua extracted juicy seeds of truth that dripped with life and made you crave the next layer of ripe beauty. Even before his time at your village came to an end, the answer was clear, you would follow. You would travel with the Rabbi and his disciples. You had intended to stay for only a week, but then one turned into two and then two turned into four. Even though you loved to hear the "Anointed One" teach, your favorite times were the evenings around the fire and walking and talking from town to town.

On this day, Yeshua prepares to teach on a hillside near the Sea of Galilee. The gentle hills slope up from the sea, covered with rocks and grasses. Boats dot the shoreline, but this activity bustles away from the villages and the fish markets in town. Over several days the word traveled that the new Rabbi was here and the crowds have grown. You work with other young men to direct crowds and to help protect the teacher from the crush of the throng who await a healing touch or a story. As you look across the hills and valleys, you see people milling around, waiting for the teacher to begin. The crowd is already large but the trails of dust rising from the road promise that more people are coming.

You glance at Yeshua and find him laughing with some of the younger boys. He tousles their hair. In a moment, he stands and faces the crowd. As he rises, he greets everyone with "Shalom." Heads turn, men stop their debates in mid-sentence, mothers grab the running toddlers, wrestling youths unlock their struggle and old women silence their gossip.

Yeshua turns to the crowd with a quiet smile, takes a deep breath and starts to clap. He claps in a slow and steady beat that picks up speed as the crowd joins in. Even the children and the old men join the simple rhythm. Only the serious, rigid and angry sit silently watching the group.

As the cheerful clapping continues, the sounds of newfound drums and sticks compliment with staccato clicks and bangs. The rhythm matches the sound of the waves nearby and makes the hills vibrate with joy. As more hands join the clapping, the Messiah nods to several of the disciples who step forward and sing a familiar psalm of David. Their clear tenor voices cut through the music and like a drawstring on a bag pull all the harmonies together.

The energetic voices of the young men rise above the clapping and soon the crowd is singing the response. The song swells as more of the group join in the familiar lyrics. One song leads to the next and then a faster one makes even the oldest bounce to the rhythm.

The young men jump up and dance, leap and celebrate. The old men prance with them in dusty circles. The old women sway. The young girls twirl with joy. Hands are joined and spontaneous chains of people start to weave around like connected human vines throughout the crowd. The children imitate the dance steps with laughing leaps and grubby hands in clutched circles. Scarves, colorful fabric and palm fronds wave and snap in the air as the praises and worship float higher and higher toward the heavens.

Like the merry-makers at a wedding feast, strangers join hands, dancing and laughing. You have seen the worship at the temple in Jerusalem, which is glorious and thrilling, but this celebration is as fresh as the sea breeze that causes the long sea grasses to sway across the slopes. These familiar melodies and words have become a spontaneous expression of the heart, bodies and spirits of a people. They sing a song of remembrance. They sing a song of celebration, a song of sorrow, a song of gladness. They sing of the desert and deliverance, of barrenness and birth, the journey and the joy, the miracles and the manna, the hardship and the hope.

They sing the song of their tribe, the tribe of Israel. It is the song of identity, and of faith with long roots deeper than time. It is a sound that grows and wraps even the hardest hearts in the soft fabric of remembrance of their history as a people. In song, even the darkest prodigal and the most isolated individual are united with their forefathers and reminded of their identity.

As the many become the one, in voice and motion, Yeshua motions to an older man with a gray beard. The village father steps forward and chants a song of remembrance and blessing. The crowd stops and stills in reverence to the words of Yahweh. The song of the old man touches their hearts. As the old man finishes with a final quiver in his voice, it locks the crowd into a communal prayer of "How long, oh Lord?" With a collective sigh the multitude starts to settle in expectation of the teaching.

Again, Yeshua greets the ever-growing assembly with "Shalom, peace" – and the atmosphere shifts. Like a stone dropped in a pool of water, hushed waves of silence flow out and down the hill in every direction. Hundreds of faces and eyes lock on the Master. Having come from a small village, the sight looks amazing and feels terrifying at the same time.

So many eyes, so many faces. Some shine bright with hope. Some full of expectation. Some downcast with need. Some cautious, measuring every thought. Some praying for the keys that will open their prisons of fear. Some wait for a good story – something to entertain their friends around the dinner fire. Some eyes belie their inner pain and anger. Some appear strengthened with trust and conviction. Eyes searching for assurance, critical of every syllable. Eyes thinly veiled with jealousy and hate. Eyes wet with tears of joy. Eyes full of love, enlarged with the tender, eternal vision.

The sight of all the eyes looks overwhelming. Seeing the expectations. Watching the critics. Measuring the spectrum and the weight of needs causes you to wonder how the Master can face, much less carry this throng. But, as he stands before them, Yeshua does something touching before he speaks.

Throughout the singing and dancing, he roamed around and spoke with many. Now he smiles and steps around the group, his movements like a strong wind pushing a full sail. He takes time and looks toward the many. His eyes greet theirs. He doesn't rush, but looks at those close and far away.

He smiles at the followers and welcomes the others with a nod and word. Like the click of a door latch, a connection is made with people. It's as if he knows the names and questions in each heart before he even begins. As his gaze sweeps the area, some glance down or look away, distracted by an object that needs immediate attention.

Yeshua takes a deep breath and tells a story you have heard before, but it has changed. He speaks with passion and his gestures make him seem ten feet tall. His voice flows with expression causing ordinary phrases to sound majestic. His face lights with enthusiasm that brings every character to life. The crowd leans in and listens attentively. At times they are listening so hard that for a moment, they forget to breathe.

The story sounds so simple that even little children nod with understanding. It's so basic that even the oldest person can remember the details. The analogies are so ordinary that both the rich and poor have lived them. As the Rabbi tells the stories, God's presence feels larger than life, yet closer than truth.

Listening on this summer day, your mind and heart feel like a lump of clay in the potter's hand that is spinning faster and faster while being pulled up into an unknown form. You realize you will not walk the same path again – never again. The Rabbi Yeshua ignited a hunger for truth and a quest for the presence of God.

CHAPTER 1
COMMUNICATION PREMISES

The *On a Hill* story is how I've imagined Yeshua (Hebrew name, short form) or Jesus (Hebrew-translated-to-Greek-translated-to-English name) would teach. For centuries, talented writers, artists, actors and preachers have used their best skills to create novels, movies, pictures and teachings that portray this carpenter. The truth remains, that until we press the "giant time–warp–replay button" in heavenly places, we can only imagine or guess how Jesus sounded and how he looked. Regardless of the absence of firsthand DVD recordings of those ancient days, time and history show that Jesus and the words he spoke altered history. The focus of this book is to evaluate and learn from Jesus' communication methods. The exploration endeavors to discover universal principles and techniques that any person can incorporate to enhance communications in every area of life.

Using my training as a professional media coach and communications consultant, I examine and find several key strategies, which make up the foundation upon which the communication principles of Jesus are built. These principles stand and remain standing. In the same way scientific assumptions precede an experiment, the strategies used by Yeshua (Jesus) are explored here to provide a foundation to accelerated understanding and ultimate effectiveness.

At first presentation, the individual strategies may seem obvious, but layered together they give a new meaning, understanding and perspective to communication. It works they same way as looking at individual color swatches of peach, orange, blue and purple and then experiencing the power and emotion they evoke when viewed together in a spectacular sunset.

These principles have been developed from years in the trenches of television newsrooms and decades of study. These suggestions have been honed in thousands of training sessions with anchors, reporters, politicians, sports stars, authors and business leaders. Additionally, like a Saturday night stew, many ingredients have been added from my diverse career experiences to serve up, what I hope is a different and unique approach on the communication menu.

In growing and learning it is important to rethink the basic questions. Sometimes we don't know the answers, and that is fine. With time and understanding, we may find them. Sometimes we have an answer, but it may not be the only one. So, please take a few moments to ponder these tenets of communication, called premises here, and you will discover that like a majestic oak, the roots are deeper than the branches are wide.

PREMISE #1 – CONSIDER THE SOURCE!

The primary source for this book is the Bible. I have referenced several translations and studied the Hebrew and Greek meanings of certain terms such as: speak, talk, commune and others. The overriding challenge remains that aside from the reverence of Scripture, no one has a certified recording or original manuscript written by an eyewitness of Jesus' teachings. (Oh, how many wars would have been avoided and how much simpler it would be if we had one. But, knowing the exploitative nature of man, if we had an original, it would probably have been turned into a taxable shrine.) So, it is better that some mysteries remain hidden like buried treasures, that way we are each forced to dig for revelation and forge our faith instead of depending on a manmade punch list. We have tremendous Bible study helps, dictionaries and commentaries to use, but even the best of

translations are still adaptations from fifth, eighth or tenth generation versions, which were written in several languages.

At seminary, I was taught that the Gospels were written in
Greek or Aramaic, but current scholarship suggests that some of the
gospels (Matthew, Mark, Luke and John), which are the narrations
about the life of Jesus, may have been originally written in Hebrew
and then translated into Greek for the growing population of gentile
believers. There are many debates about the language Jesus spoke, as
it makes a difference in the way certain stories are interpreted.

My personal belief is that Jesus was multilingual, like most
people in his region. As he was very clear about being sent to the
people of Israel, logic says that he taught in Hebrew when at the
synagogues. When he interacted with the Romans or the people
who crowded around him, he used Aramaic, which was the
common language. (It is believed that Paul, even though highly
educated as a Sadducee and fluent in many languages, wrote many
of his letters in Greek, as they were directed not to the Hebrew but
to gentile communities.)

Personally, being a journalist, a compulsive note taker, and a
child of an electronic age, I still have a difficult time relating to the
nature of communication in a world based on "Oral Tradition." Jesus
lived in pre-printing press times. In Jesus' day, the average person
transmitted information orally and recalled information through
memorization. Scribes were equivalent to web masters or computer
programmers in today's job pool. But, as someone pointed out to me,
there were still lots of writing instruments, even though they may
not have survived.

Have you ever noticed in the Greek and Roman mosaics and
images from before 500 BC that scribes and the educated used little
wax tablets that they wore around their waist? These wax tablets were
the PDAs (the personal digital assistants) of the time and a standard
transcription tool for thousands of years. It would stand to reason that
if officials and scribes were among those gathered to hear Jesus speak,
someone could have transcribed some of his teachings. Even though
the gospels weren't written until decades after his death – could it be

that many of Jesus' teachings and sermons may have been recorded on location? And then just possibly repeated verbatim, before being transcribed onto more permanent materials like scrolls, clay, metal or papyrus?

There are no conclusive answers to these questions. I do not mean to imply or indicate in any way that I concur with fictitious stories and newfound gospels. The point remains – anyone studying and trying to interpret biblical texts has to consider the challenges that affected them. In spite of being filtered through time, languages, cultures and numerous translations, the brilliance of Jesus' messages and methods shine through magnificently. Even with limitation, variance and controversy over these Scriptures, volumes can be learned from what survived. In working with the simple stories and narratives, I have only begun to touch and understand the wisdom of this carpenter turned rabbi. It has been said that the Bible is deeper than it is long. So, in jumping into the depths of the gospels, there is much to be discovered from Jesus' words and the way in which he communicated them.

PREMISE #2 – COMMUNICATION IS A FOUNDATION OF HUMAN EXISTENCE

Communication is the electricity of human existence. All we do depends on communication. It is the building block, the glue, the design, the medium, the conduit, the tool through which we do, say, love, express and experience everything. It is so basic and critical that we forget how important it is until there is a problem. Just like losing your voice, cell phone or Internet connection, without communication nothing happens.

Communication defines how we relate to families, the world and to ourselves. From the most basic needs of a crying infant to the complex speeches of a campaigning politician, all share the same needs. Communication is the currency, with which we survive, succeed and celebrate. It is the fabric of society and the network we all are born into. Communication is a human need. Deprivation from communication or from our ability to receive or give it, can crush and twist the human spirit. In our modern world, apart from the death penalty, solitary confinement is the harshest form of human punishment.

Sometimes communication is a matter of will, but often there are deep-rooted experiences that bind our ability to communicate. I have a dear friend whose husband will not tell his kind and lovely wife that he loves her. Through hard work in a rough industry he climbed from the bottom to become a very successful businessman. Their marriage is stable and they are enjoying the joys of retirement and grand-children. Even after over 30 years of marriage, he seems to remain unable to give her or his children the verbal affirmation of a declaration of his love for her and for their offspring. His wife knows that her husband loves her. Nevertheless, she still hopes each day that he may find the words to say it.

Human beings were made to be in relationships, groups and in families, which depend on communication to function. The word "communication" is derived from "commune," which means to come together, to join together or to connect. It is the same root for the words community, communion and commerce. From the social to the spiritual, communication is the conduit for relationships both with one another and with God.

Through communication we also establish our individual and corporate identities. Language and expression help to

Communication – A Divine Gift

Humans have the voice box, vocal folds, muscles, lung capacity, resonating cavities and brain struc-ture that allow them to make sounds, words, and music and imbue them with meaning. Of all the mammals that walk the earth, we are the only ones with the complete linguist tool kit. Could it be that when God said, "Let Us make man in Our image, according to Our likeness" that the image of God was more than a visual shape? Perhaps that likeness included communication gifts that also reflect the "likeness of God."

– Genesis 1:26.

define who we are from our ethnic group to nationality, or to family and tribe. Every family, biological or chosen, has its own tongue and stories that are told around the dinner table, the tales that unite their hearts and minds. From the ancient text to the daily slang, how we communicate creates invisible links between all humankind.

PREMISE #3 – WORDS HAVE POWER

Life or death is in the power of the tongue.

We all have experienced the power of words both good and bad. Think of a time when someone dear to you said the words "I love you!" What did those words do to you? Were you ready to shout, dance, climb a mountain, melt or touch the stars?

Now think of a time when someone's words wounded you. Despite the years, it is often easy to recall with clarity times when we have been wounded and remember the lies that pierced our souls. We all have dealt with negative words and, hopefully, have learned to forgive and grow beyond the experience.

The definition of "word" is described as a unit of language which is composed of one or more units call morphemes. Morph is the root of words such as "metamorphosis" which means transformation. The term comes from the Greek word meaning "shape" or "form." On the passive side of descriptions, morph is also the root for "Morpheus" the Latin god of dreams. This is

Breath of Life

Genesis tells us that when the Lord spoke the universe responded and things were created. It was in response to "the living word" or logos, that the worlds were created. When God made man and woman He breathed and made a living being. One of the definitions in the Hebrew texts of this "breath of life" was that God made man a "speaking spirit". So, did the breath of God give man the ability to communicate?

– Genesis 2:7

how the heroine-based drug, morphine, got its name because it makes people sleepy and listless.

Like a single raindrop, an individual word may not have much power. It joins other words to create a flow of sounds, which convey a strand of meaning. When the individual strands and words are woven together like a basket, they create messages and stories that carry facts or feelings, truths or lies. Words give form to thoughts, which in turn shape beliefs, which result in actions or inactions. Words can be a catalyst for change or a door to inertia. Words cause people to strive for greatness or be frozen by fear.

Spoken or Written Words – Which Hurts More?

It's interesting to consider – why do spoken words seem to hurt more than the written ones? Is it that we can hear the audio replay in our heads longer than when we read the words of a Dear John letter? This demonstrates the impact of a spoken word and the added dimensions of meaning and emotion that a human voice gives to a word.

Three Signals People Remember

Research tells us that from a standard one-on-one conversation there are three signals that people remember. The three are the words spoken, the visual appearance and the auditory message. The auditory message is distinct from the words. It is what a voice sounds like and includes the pace, tone, volume, pitch, inflection, which add meaning to the words. This is how people remember:

What People Remember	
Visual	55%
Auditory	38%
Words	7%
Total	100%

This study reveals that people watch and listen more to your presentation than they pay attention to the words or what you are actually saying. These multiple signals can either work together or can distract (what we call mixed signals). We all have experienced misunderstandings that have come from people reacting to the way we said something rather than the actual words. This is a very common problem with husbands and wives – women typically react emotionally to the way something is said. Men are baffled because they focus on their words, not realizing their tone said, "I'm bored." The principle to remember is the way words are presented makes an impact. It either charges the listeners or lulls them to sleep.

PREMISE #4 – THE UNIVERSAL FEAR OF PUBLIC COMMUNICATION

Fear is the mind killer.
– Frank Herbert, *Dune*

Imagine that you are in a critical business meeting. Your boss turns to you and asks you to answer a question. Whoops, you don't know the answer. How do you feel? Does your stomach twist into pretzels? Does your mouth get dry? Does your chest feel tight? Does your breathing become shallow? Does your throat clench slightly so that when you start to speak the pitch of your voice is elevated – or even worse, it cracks a little? For hours and days afterward do you replay the situation and punish yourself for what you should have said but were unable to say because your mind was frozen with fear? These are some of the common symptoms of stage fright, which are, at one time or another, shared by everyone.

Communication is one of the most basic drives, yet it is the greatest fear of all. It is amazing that research consistently shows that the number one fear people have is of public speaking and communicating in public. This means that the fear of communication is greater than the fear of death, loss of a child, a spouse, a job or failing health! Why is this so? What are we afraid of?

COMMUNICATION TRAUMA

Most people will tell you they are afraid of making a mistake, being ridiculed, judged or perceived as inadequate because of their lack of skill. Practice helps people develop communication skills and there are hundreds of courses, media coaches and groups such as Toastmasters that provide support. But even though people rehearse, practice and drill, many still wrestle with fear.

The main reason is that people have emotional and mental insecurities, or fears, that don't go away with simple practice and a few tricks. The core issue is that communication is more than words. True communication comes from the very essence of who we are. People are afraid of public speaking not because of the words, but they are afraid they will be judged and rejected by others. People want to be respected and admired. How people perceive the image that we project affects our self-esteem and our security. Or in simple words, we want people to like, respect and love us. But where does this fear come from and how does it grow?

Before they have words, infants know how to communicate their needs vocally and physically. As children grow, they become dancers, singers, artists, actors and storytellers. Children make a game of communicating from the simple peek-a-boo to the pronouncement of bodily functions in public places. They learn to use an inside voice and to join with others reciting the alphabet. Children make us laugh with their play acting and refresh us with their joy of expression.

But something happens in the growth process that changes the freedom and love of communication. We teach children and adults how, when and what to communicate by the responses we, and others, give them. Sometimes response teaches appropriate behavior. Other times we teach socialization or cultural morays.

CULTURAL MESSAGES – DON'T CRY, DON'T HIT!

Boys are taught, "Big boys don't cry." Anger and hitting is ok for sports. Girls are taught not to hit or be angry. We teach girls to use tears to get what they want. At school, many are teased by peers or rejected for succeeding. Siblings or friends mock other children. This and many other wounds cause children and all of us to modify our behavior. If we don't adjust to the pressure, we suffer the pain of rejection, abandonment or public ridicule.

Looking from a universal window are communication fears simply part of the essential struggle against the world? Like the caterpillar to the butterfly, must each soul embrace this struggle in order to fly into their destiny? At some level, is the communication battle an individual's fight for truth against falsehoods, good against evil, right against wrong, light against darkness? And if so, why are people wounded and attacked in this area at such an early age?

Regardless of positive reinforcement given by parents, family or friends, most people learn to fear the consequences of public communication. One reason is the lack of reinforcement for normal communication. In sports and the performing arts, people are cheered and applauded. Success and victory receive immediate affirmation and encouragement.

Often communication gifts are the most envied and the most readily attacked by those around us. Imagine a child reciting a perfect lesson who is mocked by an older brother. Classmates laugh at a student reading out loud. An employee who gives a solid presentation is criticized in jealous whispers by co-workers. In a meeting for the local charity, the bold voice of the young administrator with new ideas meets cold silence and condescending resistance.

In working with thousands of people, I have observed that many of today's greatest communicators have one thing in common. Each of them experienced challenges in their past that they had to overcome to speak successfully. For example, what issues do actor James Earl Jones and Pastor Tony Evans have in common? Both have had speech challenges. Others have had to overcome abuse or extreme adverse circumstances to push through to their destiny, such as Oprah Winfrey and best-selling author Frank Perretti. But this is not unusual. Moses, Isaiah, Jeremiah and Paul all wrote of their fear of public speaking and complained that they were "slow of speech."

To become great at it, all have to face the fear of communication. For everyone, it is a matter of pushing past the rejection, criticism, lies and opinions of others until we can uniquely express ourselves. Think of what Jesus overcame – poverty, a blue-collar background and dubious parentage (after all, he was considered a bastard to many in his community).

Regardless of who we are or what our backgrounds may be, everyone has to deal with the fear of communication on several levels. Through understanding the rules of communication, preparation, rehearsal and mental focus, most people find success in public speaking. The rule is that 70% of nervousness can be eliminated through preparation and rehearsal. Remember that like any other skill, communication requires practice to improvement.

PREMISE #5 – COMMUNICATION IS LIKE A BEHAVIOR PATTERN

When was the last time you tried playing a new sport, video game or musical instrument? Were you great the first time up to bat or on the microphone? Or did you take time to practice at home or by yourself before jumping on the field?

This is the way I feel at the start of ski season. My first day on the slopes I like to take some of the beginner runs alone so I can rediscover my balance and wipeout as needed. When I first started skiing, I had friends who told me to simply visualize myself going down the mountain and it would help keep me from falling. Great theory, but no matter how hard I "think skiing" I have to "do skiing" in order to succeed. It takes several times up and down the mountain for me to relearn the unnatural behavior of sliding down slippery slopes so I don't endanger innocent bystanders and friends with my lack of athletic prowess.

Communication is a skill and, like any other physical skill, requires training of behavior patterns. We all have communication behavior patterns, both conscious and unconscious. But to change a behavior pattern takes focus and time. Some can be changed quickly like learning to buckle your seat belt, but others, like changing your eating habits, take more time and concerted effort. When we change, it usually feels uncomfortable because it is different. That is when we need others to reinforce and help us continue to correct the new behavior.

Jesus used many behavior patterns and techniques in communication. Once you understand them and how to integrate them, remember it will take time and practice to succeed. Growth is a process so give yourself time to integrate the suggestions in the following chapters and don't try to do everything at once.

PREMISE #6 – PEOPLE COMMUNICATE ON MULTIPLE LEVELS SIMULTANEOUSLY

The five-year-old daughter of a friend came into the kitchen to tell her mother something important. Mom was occupied preparing dinner. With her eyes on the cutting board, she asked her daughter what she wanted. Again the five-year-old said, *"Mommie, I want you to listen to me."* The mother, still working on the meal, replied, *"Honey, I am listening to you. What is it?"*

Then the five-year-old insisted, *"Mommie, I want you to listen to me with your eyes."* The mom set down her knife, turned and looked at her daughter as she spoke.

The way we speak and listen requires more than just our ears. It involves all of our senses, intellect and intuition. We can often tell what is going on even when we don't hear the words. For example, have you ever walked by a room and heard people talking in elevated voices? Without knowing the people or the words, you know immediately whether they are happy, angry or afraid because of the emotion in their voices.

Just as our brain is able to multi-task, we are able to communicate on multiple levels at the same time. We call this multi-track communication. It is the subject of Chapter Seven. When you think about all of the individuals in a crowd, how did Jesus do it? How did he reach across socio economic bridges and into the corporate heart of a mismatched fickle group of people? He did it with some S.I.M.P.L.E.™ techniques that were rooted in understanding of the needs of others and in speaking truth at all times.

Premise #7 – Culture Influences Communication

Jesus was a reflection of his culture. He was Hebrew. He grew up in a rural area outside of an influential city. Communication is a product of the many dimensions of who we are. This book is filled with expressions that reflect my nationality, gender, work experience, entertainment choices, interests and humor (some good and some a little corny). Jesus' words, stories, parables, allegories, similes, images and expressions all reflect who he was and the culture in which he lived. Some of the expressions he used can only be understood within the context of the Hebrew culture.

One example is the saying, "If your eye is evil, then your body will be filled with darkness. If your eye is good, then your body will be filled with light." For years, I thought that an evil eye meant a curse. In fact, an evil eye meant stingy. Good eye meant generous.[1] This is just one of many such examples of misinterpretations to be addressed. To the best of my ability I am trying to comprehend Jesus' communication technique through the eyes of his culture.

There are challenges with this approach. Jesus was a participant of both culture and counterculture at the same time. He was of it, but not controlled by it.

What about the Jewish roots of Christianity? Many gifted scholars have addressed this debate and I defer to the work of Dr. Daniel Juster, Asher Intrater, Ray Vander Laan, Dr. David H. Stern and many others.[2] My personal opinion is that if something starts as an olive tree then it continues as an olive tree. The branch that is grafted to the established tree only lives because of the life of the older tree.

Did Jesus Use Humor?

Without a doubt, I believe that Jesus used humor in his stories. The first reason is because the exaggeration of character flaws is one of the foundations of comedy. The parables demonstrate Jesus using this element.

[1] Matthew 6:22-23. According to Dr. David H. Stern, Jesus was quoting a proverb that in Judaism good meant generous and stingy meant bad. The Greek translation and other interpretations of this implied bad or evil eye, which was not congruent with the context. Page. 32. The *Jewish New Testament Commentary*, Jewish New Testament Publications, Clarksville, MD, 1992.
[2] These authors and many others have written some excellent books on the topic. Many of which provided invaluable material for this project.

The second is based in the observation of crowds. Jesus was incredibly popular. He had command of an audience who tracked him across water and wilderness. They sat for hours with their children in rural areas without fast food or porta-potties. This sort of dedication makes no sense unless the journey proved worth the time and effort. People don't sit for hours listening to things that are boring and make them feel sad. No one commands the love and affection of an audience without using humor and making people laugh. Humor is the shortest distance between people – think Bob Hope, Carol Burnett, Bill Crosby and Jerry Seinfeld.

The third reason I believe Jesus used humor is observation of the entertainment industry. An overwhelming majority of classic comedy writers for stage and screen have been Jewish. This Jewish cultural gift for storytelling and humor has touched and changed the world. I believe that Jesus had the gift and used it to expose ungodliness in leaders. They say that the pen is mightier than the sword. Humor can be more damaging then a canon. Humor is the quickest way to shine a light on the silliness and inconsistencies of leaders. To those of his time, Jesus' stories must have made them shake their heads and laugh at the same time. Even though the humor has not been recorded, I believe Jesus used humor in his stories because it is a great defensive tool.

God writes a lot of comedy...the trouble is, he's stuck with so many bad actors who don't know how to play funny. – Garrison Keillor

JESUS AND THE CULTURE OF QUESTIONS

Jesus was a reflection of his time, culture, education and beliefs. Taking all of these into consideration and adding the typical communication blessings of Hebrews helps give context for the way Jesus used interactive tools. Questions are a common practice and sophisticated technique in the rabbinical and Middle-Eastern mindset. Questions are an integral tool for all great teachers, regardless of culture. Consider how Aristotle or Confucius used questions and riddles that are read continually in philosophy books and fortune cookies. (If it was a competition for pervasive impact, I think that Confucius definitely won.)

This "culture of questions" an ongoing part of today's Jewish culture. It has impacted history and touches lives today, especially in the media venues. Consider journalists – Ted Koppel, Barbara Walters, Larry King and hundreds of authors, print, radio and magazine writers – who are always asking questions. Their approach helps us understand our world and helps to keep leaders accountable.

On the positive side of the question spectrum is the power and perplexity of life that writers and comedians share with us. How we love and appreciate the humor of talents such as Billy Crystal, Jerry Seinfeld, Groucho Marx, Gilda Radnor, or Mel Brooks. In the Jewish culture, family members joke about the way a parent answers a question with a question.

For example:

How do you feel, ok?   Reply: Do I look like I feel ok?
What are you doing?   Reply: What do you think I should be doing?
Where have you been? Reply: What does it matter to you?
Do you need anything? Reply: Why should you care if I'm dying?

Now, if these questions feel familiar, not to worry, guilt is an equal opportunity parenting tool. It can be used by any race or religion.

Some believe that the best humor comes from overcoming hardship, poverty and rejection. Regardless, when it comes to making the best out of emotional stress, like Rapunzel trapped by circumstances, Jewish comedians have spun their problems, anxieties and insecurities into box office gold. On a broader scale, out of this "culture of questions" the greatest films, televisions shows, networks and studios have been born.

Some people have asked if the appeal of these comedians was more from the New York boroughs rather than their Jewish roots. This is a good observation, but with the right script, the Manhattan misfit is as humorous as the legally blond California girl. In spite of the New York accents, the timing and the jokes would have never worked without universal appeal.

In a recent *Strategic Business Communication Training*,[3] I asked the group of mostly non-Americans to describe their jobs. One of the women from Taiwan said her job was like a Jerry Seinfeld episode in that every day was a crisis and nothing ever happened. It was interesting how, regardless of birth nation, every person in the group was able to passionately relate to an American sitcom and talk about the characters as if they were their own family.

The production ranks of Hollywood and the major television networks are rapidly involving more women and more minorities. Still the "DNA of questions" and the foundation rules for writing, humor, and scripting are clearly established within the community. Personally, I believe that there is something about having a culture of questions that provides a genetic inheritance for media success. If I could bottle it and patent it, I would. Until then, we have to study those who knew how to ask the right questions.

EMPOWERED COMMUNICATION IS THE GOAL

Since the Tower of Babel, men and women have had more communication differences than similarities. Languages, culture, gender, personalities and experiences must be bridged in order to have genuine connection. Communication is more than a work of the soul and action of the will. At its best, it connects all parts and levels of man into a focused and positive force.

Every person communicates best when simply being himself/herself. The goal of this book is to help people learn how to empower communication with a whole brain, whole person, wholehearted and whole spirit approach. The amazing thing is that, even though this sounds difficult, the more we understand and start to use the techniques of Jesus, the simpler and easier it is to master communication.

---

[3] SBCT stands for Strategic Business Communication Training developed by EmPowercom.Us.

CHAPTER 2
WHAT IS A MASTER COMMUNICATOR?

Imagine one who possesses the combined communication skills of Larry King, Steven Spielberg, Ted Koppel and Matthew Broderick. What a dynamic person that would be! Unbelievable, yes. Incredible, most assuredly. Impossible, no, but definitely rare.

When I imagine what the communication skills of Jesus, the Messiah, must have been like, the combined skills of these gifted Power Communicators provides only a starting point. These four men utilize different forums, but they all excel in their individual sector of influence. They have distinctly different communication strengths; put them together and you have a terrific compass that charts a range of communication styles.

WHAT MAKES A MASTER COMMUNICATOR?

When you hear the definition of a Master Communicator, who comes to mind? It could be a news anchor, a politician, an actor, a radio personality, a musician, a sportscaster, a pastor, an author, an advertising executive, a film director, a teacher or a business leader.

Now imagine listening or watching this Master Communicator. What is he or she like? What makes him or her great? What does he do that demands your attention or grips your heart? How does she shape the message? How does this person use stories and information? How does she craft fit them together? How does he make you feel? And what do you remember afterward?

Can you see and hear the person? Now take a moment and write down a few things that describe this person's communication attributes. How does his message sound? Was she prepared? Is he believable? Relaxed? Confident? Humorous or serious? Sincere?

Examine the communication tools these gifted people use. Look at his or her presentation. Notice the body language and the expressions. How do they use their voice and inflection? What do the eyes say?

What is the level of skill? How about believability and confidence? How well is the message imparted? What do you remember afterward? How much do you remember the next day, week, month or year?

I have posed these questions to thousands of people. The responses about the characteristics of a Master Communicator come out the same.

Here are a few terms people use to describe a Master Communicator:

Confident, strong, memorable, easy to listen to and follow, great stories, very real, believable, credible, authoritative, intelligent, commanding, life-changing, inspirational, animated, dynamic, great expressions, focused, prepared, energetic; you get the picture.

PRESENTATION ATTRIBUTES OF A MASTER COMMUNICATOR

DESCRIBE A GREAT PRESENTER	
Energetic	Confident
Interesting	Knowledgable
Warm	Real
Memorable	Multi-faceted
Good voice	Strong
Attractive	Storyteller
Eye contact	Well paced
Good posture	Informative
Compelling	Easy to listen to

Research Helps Determine Success

In our media saturated world, research is often used to determine what will be successful and shapes everything from toothpaste commercials and evening news anchor teams to sitcom stars and clothing design. Research is an excellent tool for predicting what the audience may immediately dislike. It is not as successful in prophesying what will win the hearts of the public and predicting the long-term impact that a certain personality may have. While research may not predict who will be a Master Communicator, research does indicate which people and messages connect and evoke positive audience response.

TEN CHARACTERISTICS OF A MASTER COMMUNICATOR

History and time are the best indicators of a person's rating on the influence meter. Though it is everyone's goal to develop and project excellent communication, receiving the prize for Master Communicator takes time, aptitude, and development.

Consider the lives and accomplishments of Master Communicators like William Shakespeare, Confucius, Benjamin Franklin, Winston Churchill, Mother Theresa, Abraham Lincoln, Martin Luther King, Queen Elizabeth, Mahatma Gandhi, Florence Nightengale, Thomas Edison, Margaret Thatcher, Mark Twain and Jesus of Nazareth. Regardless of their time, culture and message, they all shared universal principles of communication that provided the platform for their success, established their position, fueled their momentum, transformed paradigms and impacted the human experience. They all became historical and timeless icons.

Regardless of the time, culture and sphere of influence, ten common communication characteristics contribute to the success of Master Communicators.

CHARACTERISTICS OF A MASTER COMMUNICATOR

Relational

Bridge Builder

Birthing the New on the Past

Establishes New Truth

Fresh Images and New Vocabulary

Focused and Congruent

Humble

Quotable

Relational Paradigm Shifts

Reproduces Values

1. RELATIONAL AND "OTHER FOCUSED"

A Master Communicator is a true servant leader. People know when a leader, teacher, minister or journalist truly cares about them. This genuine concern causes a positive response in the hearer. A Master Communicator's focus is directed toward the needs of others rather than on decorating his own billboard. Mother Teresa loved the poorest of the poor. Benjamin Franklin loved America before it was born. Martin Luther King loved people and equality, and he stood for freedom. Jesus loved and healed many individuals.

We must combine the toughness of the serpent and the softness of the dove, a tough mind and a tender heart. – Martin Luther King Jr.

2. BRIDGE BUILDER

Master Communicators know how to build bridges so others can cross divides into new understanding. In the human experience there are great divides of social, political, economic, spiritual, cultural and gender issues. Communicators are like bridges or ambassadors who help others traverse the canyons of understanding.

A Master Communicator builds bridges. These can connect different groups, which creates new alliances, opportunities, and industries. Other bridges stretch vertically, from the heights of heaven to the streets of man, or from the privileged to the needy.

Abraham Lincoln helped unite Americans with "Government of the People, by the People and for the People." Alexander Graham Bell provided inventions such as the telephone, which enabled people to talk to anyone, anywhere, anytime. Jesus built a bridge from heaven to earth, so that even the least could call the Almighty their "Abba" or Daddy.

In 1931, Charlie Chaplin and Albert Einstein drove down a street together. Pedestrians waved and cheered. Chaplin explained: *"The people are applauding you because none of them understands you, and applauding me, because everybody understands me."* Even though Einstein could help explain the universe, Chaplin's films were a bridge that connected the hearts of men and nations with laughter.

3. BIRTHING THE NEW ON THE PAST

Like the branches of a tree touching the sky that are strengthened by the roots in the earth below, new movement or revolution reaches to the future but has foundational roots in the past. Without the structure or financial provision of the preceding generation a new movement might dissipate before completion. Without the familiarity of known systems, social reform might unravel midway through the process and be rejected by the citizens. This may happen when the changes seem too radical and cause discomfort and fear. Reform is overturned when people prefer the comfort of the familiar past even though it might not be the best decision. For example, a military coup succeeds but after a few months of economic hardship there is unrest, which leads to a reversal and reseating of the previous leadership.

Just as a civilization is built upon the knowledge of the preceding generations, spiritual beliefs and covenants evolve with time and understanding. Jesus explained that His teachings were built upon the familiar Hebraic laws, Scriptures and words of the prophets.

Master Communicator King David's abilities included song writing and poetry. Arthur Burk explains the contribution and radical change that David brought to the temple.

David was chosen by God to introduce a new facet of worship into the stream of religious history. For 500 years there was no worship with music in the tabernacle. There were sights, sounds, smells, ceremonies, clothing, and routines of worship that pleased God but not musical worship. God waited over 500 years for his man to have the creativity to introduce music as worship. David was that man. When David tried to bring up the ark the first time, he had all kinds of musicians, but he violated the way that God had prescribed that the ark would be moved. In his excitement about embracing the new good thing, he ignored the old, and God judged the process. Later David stood on the foundation of the old and obeyed the commands to carry the ark on staves on the shoulders of the priests. He stood on the righteous foundation of the past, without violating it, and then he added worship, the new thing he wanted to introduce.[4]

4. ESTABLISHES NEW TRUTHS AND REMEMBERS FORGOTTEN TRUTH

Have you ever had a dirty windshield or a smudged pair of glasses, but didn't notice it? After cleaning them off, it is amazing to discover how much better you can see. A Master Communicator has the ability to illuminate truth in a way that is like cleaning off the dirty windshield. She helps people see with new and clear vision. Sometimes it is as simple as cleaning off the lies that are smeared on the windshield, other times a Master Communicator provides a new level of understanding. The truth may apply to any area from government to medicine, or from family to culture.

[4] Burk, Arthur and Gunter, Sylvia. *Blessing Your Spirit. With the Blessings of Your Father and the Names of God.* Published by The Father's Business, Birmingham, AL, 2005; page 57, Day 22.

Mahatma Gandhi shook the foundations of the British Empire with a simple food fast that forced people to reexamine and redefine policies. Galileo made discoveries about the solar system, which offended the religious establishments. Florence Nightingale taught that the microscopic could be deadly. Jesus redefined the truth of relationships with God, and between men, groups and genders.

5. Uses Fresh Images and New Vocabulary

Can you identify who authored these statements? "I have a dream." "Would a rose by any other name smell as sweet?" "When in the course of human events," "Are you going to Scarborough Fair?" "Now, for the Top Ten!"

I love reading quotes and discovering who crafted them.

The previous credits go to: Martin Luther King, William Shakespeare, Thomas Jefferson, Simon and Garfunkel, and David Letterman.

Great communicators know how to use words and language with artistic flair. They are able to introduce new images, analogies, metaphors, stories and vocabulary in dynamic and unforgettable ways.

Before the Satellite-Internet world could make someone famous in hours, historical people depended on simpler tools – books, traditions, legends, and artifacts – to broadcast into the future. Regardless of the time and culture, a Master Communicator is more than a "word smith" he is a "word maestro" who composes dynamic images. He is a "language artist" who paints magical stories that pour into the stream of conversation and float into the unending sea of human interaction.

Every man's life is a fairy tale, written by the fingers of God.
– Hans Christian Anderson

6. Focused and Congruent

One of the biggest challenges to communication effectiveness is an unfocused presentation and disjointed message. Sometimes people unintentionally send mixed messages. If I state that I am confident but I am slouching when I say it, my posture makes me seem insecure. It disagrees with my statement. If I don't look at you when I shake your hand, I seem afraid or timid. Not talking in a clear voice can project an image of insecurity. Mumbling can be interpreted as lack of initiative or disdain toward management.

A Master Communicator has the ability to unify all of the communication signals so the message is focused and reaches the target. A unified message is effective because it reduces the audience's distractions. A Master Communicator always keeps an eye on the goal and manages the information flow.

We can do no great things—only small things with great love.
– Mother Teresa

7. HUMILITY – MESSAGE NOT MESSENGER

When you look at a picture in a gallery, which do you notice first, the work of art or the frame? Think again, can you recall the specific detail of the frames surrounding the pictures in someone's office that you visited? If you can, you are either a gifted designer, bored with the meeting, or the artwork was hideous.

When news anchors read the headlines your focus is on the information not the anchor. Even though it is important that the person be attractive and well groomed, he is not to detract from the content of the news stories. Master Communicators know that the information and message is important, not themselves. Mother Teresa used to say, "I am simply a pencil in the hand of the Lord." Jesus claimed that he could only say what the Father said and do what the Father showed him.

When it comes to imparting the message, great communicators will defer to the mission, even though they may be egotistical when out of the spotlight. They help all eyes focus on the goal, to catalyst change and build cultural transformation.

Eating words has never given me indigestion.
– Winston Churchill

8. MEMORABLE AND QUOTABLE

One of the fastest indicators that a person may be a Master Communicator is how quickly they are quoted and re-quoted. In a research focus group, participants will be asked if they recall any advertising slogans or commercials. The most valued responses come when people recall a commercial or a tag line without being prompted. This means the ad campaign works, making the product one that has reached the mental desktop. People who excel at communication create new images and vocabulary that the public uses in daily life. When I train media professionals or speechwriters, I call this "Mental Velcro," meaning that it sticks in a person's mind and can be easily recalled.

Jesus used terms like "Love your neighbor," "Be Reborn," "the first shall be last and the last shall be first," "give to Caesar what is Caesar's!" Here are a few other phrases that are common in our culture, see if you can guess where they originated.

Don't burn the candle at both ends.

If the cap fits then wear it. (Also if the shoe fits then wear it.)

Don't put the cart before the horse.

The kit (kitten) is like the cat. (Child is like the mother. Apple doesn't fall far from the tree.)

Don't cut off your nose to spite your face.

He who cannot curb his temper carries gunpowder in his bosom, and is neither safe for himself or his neighbors. (He's carrying a loaded gun.)

When passion comes in the door, then whatever good sense there is indoors, flies out the window.

I found all of these quotes in an antique book my mother gave me. In it I found the origins of many popular sayings. The famous preacher C.H. Spurgeon created these sayings in the 1880s. Every week I hear the words of this Master Communicator echoing through daily conversation.[5]

9. CREATES PARADIGM SHIFTS AND RELATIONSHIP CHANGES

Every Master Communicator has a mission from which the messages evolve. The information can be compared to the

[5] Spurgeon, C.H., *John Ploughman's Pictures or, More of His Plain Talk for Plain People*, J.B. Lippincott & Co., Philadelphia, 1881.

repositioning of great geological plates in the earth's crust that cause earthquakes and tsunamis. When Master Communicators release their messages, the culture responds and things shift and change. Sometimes it is as basic as interpersonal relationships (man to man or man to woman), or as critical as man to society, man to government, or man to environment. But it can also cause spiritual shifts like Jesus who connected men to the Father or like Martin Luther who realigned man with faith and scripture.

> *The best way to know God is to love many things.*
> – Vincent Van Gogh

10. ABLE TO REPRODUCE VALUES IN OTHERS

Master Communicators are able to reproduce and transmit their values so that their beliefs or knowledge live beyond themselves. In order to accomplish this, there are two requirements. First, the leader must be able to teach and impart information to others. Second, the values must have universal and long-term merit.

No matter how remarkable the performance of a song may be, if people don't want to hear it again and won't sing along, it's a dud. Whether songs or sonnets, sermons or social reform, if they aren't reproduced they are of momentary value. The saying goes, "The proof is in the pudding," or the ending will prove if the beginning had the right stuff.

Master Communicators are levers, which cause cultural shifts, redefine paradigms, better the human condition, and most importantly reproduce their values in others. They are like a fruitful vine planted beside the streams of water whose fruit is nourishing and whose harvest never ends.

Think of Beethoven's symphonies, Jefferson's Bill of Rights, Shakespeare's stories, Aesop's fables, Mandela's reforms and Jesus' followers. Of all of the characteristics of effective communication, the final test is *the germination of a seed of truth into an orchard of ideas.* After the blush of the flower, the beauty of the fruit and the joy of the harvest have passed, it is the seed's multiplication that is the ultimate measure of communication greatness.

> *Every man dies but not all men live.*
> – William Wallace, Braveheart

What About Destructive Master Communicators?

Unfortunately as with any resource, skillful communication can be used for negative as well as positive means. Communication is a powerful tool, which has been used to manipulate, defraud, rob, steal, control, destroy, conquer and plunder individuals and nations. Extreme examples are Hitler, Stalin and Mao and the daily and shameless examples of unhealthy fast food advertising to children and sexual exploitation of teens on MTV.

One of my friends had an unfortunate experience with her infant daughter and her four-year-old son. The first words the daughter spoke were, McNonald or McDonalds. Instead of hearing "mommy" or "daddy" spring from those darling lips, this mom heard her daughter cry out, McNonald and "Fren-Fry." The older brother had taught his younger sister to cry out with him to make sure that he got to visit his favorite lunch spot with the play area.

Turn the Dial to Interpersonal

> *Children are apt to live up to what you believe of them.*
> – Lady Bird Johnson

Though every person may not become a Master Communicator, every person has the opportunity to master communication. We all remember conversations that powerfully touched our lives. All of us have made comments that, without our knowing, made a huge and lasting impact on others. Here is one example.

During my graduate school years, I set out on a summer day from the charming town of Whitefield, New Hampshire, where I met relatives who picked me up.

From the back seat of the car, I admired the perfect New England day, clear, cool and luscious green. My Uncle Bob drove with his fiancé Caroline riding shotgun. It was the first time I'd met her. We had an energetic conversation as we passed the green dappled hills toward my grandparents' beloved summer home. They brought me up to date on all the family matters and scheduled events. As the car overtook the final hill, we discussed my graduate work. Caroline turned and said, "Bob tells me that you are a person who can do anything that you put your mind to."

There was something stunning about that simple statement. My mind reeled with the awareness that my uncle thought that much of me. Could it be true?

It was as if a mirror had been placed in front of me and I could see a reflection of my abilities and talents for the first time. I felt amazed and embarrassed. Even though I tried to shrug it off, it stuck inside me. For the first time, I consciously believed that I could really succeed at a career.

Even though I had been told the same thing many times before by parents, teachers, and friends – this was the first time I actually believed it. My uncle's girlfriend had communicated the message to me masterfully.

The statement was simple but powerful. The weight of the conviction and the way it was worded caused it to pierce through all my defenses; my self-doubts and hit the bull's eye. The power of those words went into my spirit and changed me.

We all have memories like this that touched, shaped and changed us. We also have memories that are good and bad, positive and destructive. We have all received messages that caused us to simultaneously respond on many levels, resonating in our heart, mind, will and spirit. Comments and memories create emotions and plant beliefs deep in our psyche that became a part of us.

Beliefs like – I'm smart; I can do it; I'm attractive, strong, and capable; I can handle it. Then on the negative side – I'm stupid, bad, inadequate, messed up, doomed, worthless, never good enough and on and on.

Now think of someone who spoke into your life and you were changed. Was it something your parent noticed? Was there a special relative who had an encouraging word? Who first recognized the talents and capabilities that made your choose your career? Who gave you that boost when you were at a threshold of opportunity? What did they say that touched your heart, moved your mind and impacted your spirit? Did you ever thank them?

Do you remember the words? Where you were? Can you hear the sound of their voice or recall their facial expression? How did it change your decisions and life?

Was the person who spoke to you a "Master Communicator" or was it a moment of communication mastery? It might have been both, but undoubtedly it was an instance of communication power. Every person is capable of powerful communication that moves people's lives, alters bad decisions, and changes and shapes destinies.

All of us influence the world around us. Our words form a vast net of influence. We choose to use and shape how our messages are delivered. Taking a cue from the communication techniques of Jesus, by looking at his skills we can prepare properly, strengthen our content, strengthen our skills and improve our technique.

We all have been touched, shaped and influenced by people who have spoken into our lives. Whether people understood their impact or not, they shaped our lives. Words are tools that make the difference.

From the homespun everyday people, to the great communicators, each has the opportunity to mold others. Understanding the power of our words and how to express them can transform anyone of us and take us where we want to go.

You have to write the book that wants to be written. And if the book will be too difficult for grown-ups, then you write it for children.
– Madeline L'Engle

JESUS – MASTER OF THE S.I.M.P.L.E.™ METHOD

Previously mentioned "Power Communicators" such as Larry King, Stephen Spielberg, Ted Koppel and Matthew Broderick are all media stars known around the world. In his day, Jesus' life was fraught with adversity. He was raised in obscurity, received a basic education, operated in a tradesman environment, and enjoyed no family status, financial advantage or influential friends.

Yet, he mastered communication – through ordinary, simple, common skill that astonished the rich, the powerful, the religious, the established, the privileged and the professional.

Jesus was a brilliant communicator. Few people in history have had the impact or demonstrated such capability without the benefit of the electronic media. He accomplished all of this before the age of 34. So how did he do it? What made him different than all other communicators? The short answer is to say he was God. The more challenging answer is to look closely and evaluate what we know of his work and teachings.

In evaluating Jesus' methods of communication there are six distinct techniques that he uses over and over again. His approach, message development, presentation, imagery and audience interaction reflect what we modern day consultants and media experts identify as the distinct principles and structure of classic communication theory. I have termed Jesus' approach the "S.I.M.P.L.E. Method," which stands for the techniques of: Stories, Interaction, Multi-Track, Preparation, Love and Execution.

We have all heard that Jesus called some of the first disciples with the words, "Come with me and I will make you fishers of men." What a terrific hook! The advertising world calls this a "Branding Statement." But returning to the fishing image, the S.I.M.P.L.E.™ steps are tools this Master Communicator used for soul fishing.

To apply the "Fisher of Men" analogy, here is how the different steps work together.

S		Stories and parables are like fishing lines, baskets or packages that tie together, hold and contain information so that it is easier to remember.
I		Interaction is like hooks and bait that attract, engage and pull people into the message.
M		Multi-Track means touching people on multiple levels simultaneously, which is like stretching and using a larger drag net to maximize the size of the catch.
P		Preparation defines the content, materials and way the elements within a presentation, or net, are woven together.
L		Love defines the passion, motivation and heart of the fishermen. Love provides the foundation of truth, integrity and commitment.
E		Execution is the example, focus, commitment and follow-through that make the fishing expedition a reality. Execution unites will with disciple, direction and skill so that the goal is accomplished.

Jesus told his disciples that he would make them "Fishers of Men." The S.I.M.P.L.E.™ Method defines the tools that this Master Communicator used for fishing. By applying these simple and powerful techniques, anyone can learn how to "bait their hooks" and "cast their nets" upon the oceans of the world to capture the hearts of men.

In the following chapters the steps of the S.I.M.P.L.E.™ Method are explained using scriptures and demonstrated using the presentation techniques of TV pros and journalists. Whether a high-profile CEO dealing with crisis media, a project manager, a pastor, a journalist, a teacher, a salesperson, a bible study leader or a parent, these time tested methods will help anyone shape and prepare a stronger message, ask better questions, improve listening skills, reduce communication conflict and cope with media disasters. The stories, practical examples, "insider secrets," charts and applications will teach readers how to improve their professional, presentational and personal communication skills by learning how to "Talk Like Jesus."

> **THE GREAT ILLUSION**
> **ABOUT COMMUNICATION**
> **IS THAT ...**
>
> **IT HAS OCCURRED!**

CHAPTER 3
WELCOME TO AN A.D.D. WORLD

It's everywhere! Media technology fills our world like a giant electronic nervous system. Televisions, satellites, cell phones, movies, radios, computers and wireless devices are changing the way we live, work, play and fight. Without our permission, this modern technology continues to change our lives forever, both for the better and for the worse.

Like an exotic mistress, these mediums consume our schedules through a multitude of vicarious experiences. Through them the universe of our understanding is expanding to the galaxies while, at the same time, transmitting Attention Deficit Disorder (A.D.D.) faster than the common cold. The electronic offspring – iPods, bluetooths, MP3s, Blackberrys, DVDs, just to name a few – are constantly reshaping the way we communicate, listen and learn. The Information Age and media saturated world have created new communication problems that every person, business, company and parent must deal with and conquer.

The impact of the electronic world and Information Age is a giant net connecting the sunny beaches of Malibu to the icy peaks of Mt. Everest. Satellites and batteries have given us the freedom to take our technology to the farthest reaches of the globe in an unprecedented fashion. School children can interact with astronauts in the space shuttle while a deep-sea diver calls home on mom's birthday.

This ever-expanding media web affects every country, language, socio economic group and people. It is changing the lives, habits, thoughts and the jobs of most of the world. The frantic business climate and rush-rush lifestyle have moved media gadgets from the optional-gee-whiz category into the "must-have-now critical business tool."

With so much distraction in this media saturated world, how can we hope to be heard? Never before in history has there been more information, words, and images to stimulate or confuse us. Like a global hurricane, the last thirty years have swept us all into the "Information Age" which has radically altered the rules of communication forever. This communication transformation has impacted every dimension of our lives – personal, family, business and spiritual, yet success in these critical areas still depends on how we use our communication skills and tools. **The greater the quantity of media, the more critical the crafting of the message and its presentation.**

MEDIA TECHNOLOGY – DOUBLE-EDGED SWORD

Our love affair with media technology is a huge double-edged sword. On the positive side, the advantages are phenomenal and no one wants to try to do business without a phone, fax, website and email in today's competitive business world. Modern media technology creates new jobs, stimulates businesses, provides information, builds economic strength, and makes it possible for even the smallest business owner to improve visibility and sales.

On the negative side, like any new technology, improvements always give birth to a new group of diseases. In a media-intensive world, people deal with problems like over saturation, techno-stress, media addiction and erosion of interpersonal relationships. These problems are not exclusive to the Western world. When visiting the remote, poorest parts of third world nations, TV sets are everywhere. People may not have work or food for dinner, but they can often find a way to watch their favorite programs.

When Life's a Rat Race, Get a Cat!

No one needs to tell us how busy life has become. And it is not an illusion that things continue to get faster and faster. The media-driven world has made us feel overwhelmed and always behind. It's hard to enjoy the view from a treadmill. The kids are able to adapt better than we are because all they have known is the non-stop rhythm of the Information Age. Those of us who remember a time when a family had only one television set with a limited number of channels often feel besieged at the idea of a 500 channel satellite dish. I don't know if you have experienced this overload, but there have been several times when I have walked out of grocery and department stores because I did not have the mental energy to make a decision about what I wanted to purchase. Having too many choices seems to be more exhausting than having too few.

From *Sesame Street* to MTV Mania

The truth is that more information is coming at us than ever before. In the late 70's when *Sesame Street* was first developed, experts discovered that to keep the attention span of pre-schoolers you had to change the stimulation every 12 seconds. When you compare the programs popular with the former Sesame Streeters, now Gen-Y'ers and Gen-X'ers, to those of their parents (such as MTV to *Happy Days* or perhaps *24* to *Dragnet*) it is easy to see the difference in intensity, both visually and emotionally.

The 12-second *Sesame Street* rule of the 70's and 80's has been replaced by the faster, faster, more, more world of MTV graphics. If you watch a cutting edge music video in a single second you will see up to five to 20 layers of visuals, colors and sounds. Even the news networks have gotten into the swing with headlines, ticker tape updates, maps, stock quotes and over seven visual layers on the screen. This means there has been **an increase of more than 80 to 200 times more information a second** in 20 years.

One major reason for the change is technology and computers. In fact, technology is replaced by newer technology every eighteen months. Like magic, computers multiply, compress and layer dozens of individual tracks of music, video and graphics. This means that instead of having a new stimulation every 12 seconds with Big Bird and Oscar, computers help create a herd of Big Birds and allow Oscar to sing tenor, bass and lead at the same time.

COMMUNICATION CHALLENGES IN AN A.D.D. WORLD

With all this information and stimulation it is no wonder that we occasionally have memory lapses. After all, the media world has trained people that they really don't need to remember things. The constant blaring of advertising makes it easy for us. When you hear about an event advertised on the radio, how often do you immediately write it down? Do you wait until you hear the ad again the third or fourth go round and then make a mental note?

Parents, employers and teachers find this behavior pattern created by the media culture extremely frustrating. Students and workers will often depend on another commercial or their moms or bosses to remind them about details instead of taking responsibility for their homework, actions and chores. Though it may seem minor, this behavior pattern is very destructive to the maturity of an individual. Recognizing and addressing this issue is one of many challenges created by the electronic media world.

Here are a few media statistics, which increase every month.[6]

- Annually, Americans watch **250 billion hours** of television.
- The average North American family has the TV on for **8 hours a day**. That is an hour more than a decade ago.
- In the industrialized world, individuals spend fully half of their leisure time watching television. At this rate a person who lives to 75 would **spend nine years** in front of the television.[7]
- Children see from **800,000 to 1.5 million acts of violence** by the time they are 17 years old.[8]

[6] Media usage statistics from A.C. Nielson Co.   Found on *The Sourcebook for Teaching Science*, http://www.csun.edu/science/health/docs/tv&health.html.
[7] *Television Addiction Is No Mere Methaphor*, by Robert Kubey and Mihaly Csikszentmihalyi, Scientific American, February 23, 2003, page 2.
[8] Statistics from American Pediatric Association website.

SYMPTOMS OF MEDIA OVERLOAD

There are many symptoms of media overload in our society. Just think of how your life has changed because of the media streams that run through it. Email was supposed to make our lives easier, but the reverse is true because now we have even more messages and information to juggle.

SYMPTOM #1 – I'm Dancing as Fast as I Can

Now, that I have all this technology to make my life easier – why is it that I feel like I'm further behind?

SYMPTOM #2 – Help, My Brain Needs More RAM!

With all this information coming in everyday, do you find yourself forgetting simple things like laundry, briefcases or occasionally a child?

SYMPTOM #3 – Are You Sleep Deprived Due to Channel Surfing?

How often do you find yourself or your spouse, surfing up and down the channels two, three and four times a night like an impatient desperate fisherman – trolling for that great program or classic movie that you have already seen five times? Nothing like a good rerun!

SYMPTOM #4 – Have You Felt "Slimed?"

Have you ever felt like you wanted to take a shower after watching a show, a movie or listening to certain radio hosts or songs? Have your felt dirty after seeing unexpected commercials or pop-ups flash in front of you? When the media throws junk into our brain without permission, it slimes us. It's like the movie Ghostbusters II, when the ghosts covered everyone in slime and toxic goop that sucked up all the positive energy. Sometimes I can't hit the channel changer fast enough. Hey, where is that erase button for our brain anyway and why does it only work on the important stuff like taxes?

SYMPTOM #5 – T.M.I. – "Too Much Information...Very Little Learned"

Do you feel like all the news channels are repeating the same stories over and over again? Do you feel as if you have déjà vu when you jump from newscast to newscast? Do you feel as though sometimes they give you too much intimate information?

Television has proved that people will look at anything rather than each other. – Ann Landers

FASTEN YOUR SELT BELTS – IT'S A DIGITAL WORLD

What is the bottom line impact of the media saturated world? Fasten your seat belts and catch your breath! When we think about the pace of life fifteen years ago, most agree that our lives are faster, with less time to listen, think and sleep. This shift has created imbalance and the stress is showing up in our relationships with spouses, children, friends and God. The Information Revolution has created a shift in society and the rules have changed.

The electronic media world has helped us to work smarter and faster. It has given us the freedom to work from home or from a mountaintop. It allows us to reach out to the world and interact with people across the globe. The reality is that things are only going to get faster, so we need to work smart and communicate more effectively. For the first time in history, the world is connected by a multi-layered matrix, which contains multiple layers of signals, wires, cables and codes that allow the most remote voice or event to echo around the world. The complexity of this media matrix also creates distractions, however, that can cause the most obvious of issues to be overlooked.

Many people are familiar with the phrase, "The medium is the message" by Marshall McLuhan where he explains that any technology gradually creates a new environment. We experience this transformation and the growing pains in our homes, workplaces, families and churches. What this communications pioneer also told us is that the arts and media expressions are more than self-expressive, they are prophetic.

Arts as an Alarm System

In McLuhan's book, *Understanding Media, the Extensions of Man*,[9] he explains that media is a cultural art form and "art as radar acts as 'an early alarm system,' as it were, enabling us to discover social and psychic targets in lots of time to prepare to cope with them." He also warned that too much interaction with media leads to narcissistic emotions and tendencies. One has only to look at magazine covers to know that is true.

What Is the Measure of Our Culture?

When analyzing and measuring cultures, archeologists find the richest clues in ancient writings, gravesites and garbage dumps. The mysteries of civilizations are revealed along with the customs, lifestyle, businesses and religions. A thousand years from now, what will a scientist from another planet say about our world? Will they think that we were warriors or peacemakers, higher-minded or culturally reprobate, rewarders of truth or deceit; concerned with replenishing the earth or raping its riches, family-minded or woefully independent?

TV and Computers – Modern Day Altar

If these otherworld scientists from the future were to look for clues about religious activities in our world, what would they conclude? What would be considered the places of worship? Would it be the sports stadiums, filled with cheering crowds? Or perhaps, after careful examination of our habits, they would consider the millennium man, albeit seemingly violent and barbaric in arts, to be a personally devout species.

How would they explain that every dwelling had at least one if not several altars? They might note that the average family spent over seven hours a day meditating in front of the shrines, which displayed electronic images of their gods and heroes.

Behaviors Reveal Truth

Now, even though it is ridiculous to think of a television as a

[9] McLuen, Marshall, *Understanding Media, The Extensions of Man*, N.Y, 1964.

religious altar, it is important to recognize the impact that the electronic media is having upon on our families, relationships, and churches and on the world. The infatuation and dependence on media activities has rapidly grown to steal time from other human activities, like face-to-face conversations and exercise. This subtle erosion is dangerous and difficult to detect. The media-techno driven world is having profound impacts upon every area of our lives. It has been said that our behaviors reveal what is in the heart of a man. What do the behaviors of the American people and global village tell us?

JUST CUT THE CORD! DEALING WITH MEDIA ADDICTION

Once upon a time there was a mother who was trying to get the father and the children to come to the dinner table. She had worked all day, come home, cleaned the house and fixed dinner for the family of six. The hot meal was on the table and she had made repeated calls for the family to come. Instead, the father and children remained glued to the tube, watching a humorous program.

The mother was frustrated with this oft-repeated scenario. So she decided to take matters into her own hands, grabbed a pair of scissors and cut the electrical cord for the television. Fortunately, she wasn't electrocuted, but the family did learn to come to the dinner table when they were called, at least for a few weeks.

This desperate action reflects the desire of many parents and spouses. We are a media dependant society but when does our dependency cross the line into media addiction? We are flooded with media 24/7. One girlfriend said, "Who needs birth control when he's got the remote control?"

Last winter I took an evening walk around the Times Square area in Manhattan. It was my first trip to the area in years and the visual onslaught was stunning. From every direction video screens the size of whales stretched hundreds of feet into the air. I felt like Thumbelina placed on the giant's table. Giant body parts undulated beside mountainous beverages, while ravenous motor vehicles and music raged on. The magnitude of the experience made me stop and stare like a country schoolgirl. It didn't last for long because within moments I was getting dirty looks from people walking around me. Embarrassed and shamed by my "gee whiz Toto, we aren't in Kansas anymore" response, I was swept along in the madding crowd. It was astonishing how oblivious the dinner crowd was to all the free entertainment.

AROUND THE WORLD IN 60 SECONDS OR LESS.

In addition to the media flood, our world is impacted by the speed of communication. We love speed and computer memory and we just can't seem to get enough of it. The Internet has given the world immediate access to information, stories, pictures and tools that make us smarter, faster and richer. The convergence of media means that things are faster and access easier. The good news is that critical information is available; the bad news is that incorrect, false, and destructive information flies around the net even faster. This means that if you are in the public eye, you have to be prepared with talking points, media training, and public relations material, because the response time of news organizations is instantaneous.

FOURTH ESTATE TAKES THE LEAD

Whoever can speak, speaking now to the whole nation, becomes a power, a branch of government, with inalienable weight in law making, in all acts of authority. It matters not what rank he has, what revenues or garnitures. The requisite thing is, that he have a tongue, which others will listen to; this and nothing more is requisite.
– Thomas Carlyle, *On Heroes and Hero Worship* (1841)

The press has been called the "Fourth Estate" because of the influence and power that it has upon society. The challenge in today's world is that with technological advancements, media has expanded beyond the wildest visions of our founding fathers and mothers.

We are impacted by our dependence on media, the amount that we are exposed to and the content of what is carried on it. However, there is another cultural change and stress that has been created by our media-rich environment – Trial by Media. Even though rejection, slander, gossip and public shunning are parts of all societies, nothing in all of human history equates to the cumulative impact of this experience, made possible by the convergence of modern media.

TRIAL BY MEDIA

Dragged into the courts of opinion, a fair trial is a fleeting illusion. Early in my career, I was involved in a media firestorm and slandered by every major network, talk show and newspaper.

Once upon a time, I was assigned to help a new female anchor who was transitioning from a smaller California station to a midwestern market. It was a difficult assignment because, having relatives from Kansas City, I was concerned that a midwestern audience might not accept this woman's style. I expressed my reservations to my boss, but being the newest team member (and the only female), I was overruled and told that my job was to make it work.

A great deal of energy was spent helping the anchor team improve their presentation, teamwork and appearance. In fact, during that time period, more of my time was spent helping her succeed with than any other individual client. Unfortunately, after several ratings periods, the numbers were underwhelming and even worse, the station had received a large volume of negative mail about the female anchor. After conducting research, the station management made a change. The female anchor was demoted to a reporter position without a serious reduction in salary. The news director told me he hoped, with time and viewer support, that she might be able to regain the position.

Unfortunately, the female anchor decided to quit, claiming sexual discrimination. She told the world that she was fired because "she was too old, unattractive and non-deferential to men." Great line, huh? Unfortunately it was a lie, but it made great press. Repeated like a mantra, even the darkest lie starts to glimmer and the boldest reporters become paralyzed by fear.

When all the media coverage started, rather than fighting the lies, allegations, television news bashing, slander and distortions, my bosses decided to turtle down and wait for the storm to pass. My bosses let me and another researcher be slammed repeatedly by the female anchor and her spin. We were the sacrificial lambs that caught the shrapnel so that the bosses could protect the client list, which included the news-consulting contract for CBS-owned-and -operated stations.

At that time, most of the network news departments used outside consultants and researchers for their rapidly growing news divisions. The hitch was, like many corporations, they would never acknowledge the relationship in public or print. The financial revenues from the news ratings were so high that consulting companies had to stay hidden and work like stealth agents to uncover market trends and find the best talent. Our bosses feared that if they got too much news exposure from the trial, they might lose the bigger clients' contracts. To protect all of our jobs, the decision was made to sacrifice a few for the many.

Even though sexual discrimination in the news industry was an important issue, this was the wrong case. In the trial, it was exposed that station management never spoke the famous "too old, unattractive, and non-deferential to men" line. It was a fabrication. In the court of public opinion, the former anchor did an excellent job presenting her case. (Apparently, she benefited more from the coaching sessions than she would acknowledge.) In the process of the trial, we were told that this was the second time she had sued a television station. Apparently, she had gotten a settlement from the previous station. This time the court ruled against her.

Like many a media circus, more was lost than gained. Though a few had fame, for the majority, careers were devastated, energy was wasted and those on the frontlines were traumatized for years.

What did I learn during my trial by media? More than I ever wanted. Trial by media can mean that truth is not important, only the ratings matter. The better and more dramatic the quote, the more coverage is gathered. The reality is that, without internal integrity and a system of checks and balances, truth is shaped and history redefined by the media-at-large. We live in a world with dark and light where media-mongers sweep issues up and twist them more than Category 5 tornado. Fastest and first does not always equal the best and accurate.

Personally, I am grateful that my media trial occurred before the current proliferation of talk shows that masquerade as journalism. Please understand that I am deeply appreciative and respect the thousands of credible and hard working journalists in the media. They deserve more honor and attention. Unfortunately the pressures of stockholders and ratings battles have spawned info-tainment shows that "Demonize for Dollars" with "We'll be the Judge and Jury" attitudes.

WORD OF MOUTH STILL COUNTS

With the explosion of media outlets and communication channels advertisers have discovered that it is still difficult to reach people with their message. With the ability to skip commercials and on-demand programming, advertisers are developing more creative ways to reach the public. But, the more things change, the more things remain the same – especially when it comes to attracting an audience, whether it is a TV show, music group, novel or a movie.

Where blockbuster movies are concerned, aside from all the ads and movie trailers, there is one critical competent that every studio and movie star prays for: word-of-mouth response. If people like a film and tell their friends about it, then chances are a film will be a hit. Without the momentum that positive word-of-mouth provides, even the most creative endeavors fall flat.

This example proves that no matter how much our lives are impacted by technology, there is nothing more powerful than a successful exchange through one-on-one conversation. The challenge is how to reach through the filters and distractions so that people hear and understand our true message.

In a world without technology, word-of-mouth is the primary communication conduit. This is how Jesus built his following and touched so many lives, so quickly. He understood the stages of communication and through his stories and techniques, instantly built bridges to reach others.

UNDERSTANDING THE COMMUNICATION CYCLE

The single biggest problem in communication is the illusion that it has taken place. – George Bernard Shaw

This quote expresses the difficulty and challenge of any communication situation. How do we make sure people have heard, have understood and will respond? Just because a mother tells her child to do something does not mean that it is heard or done. There are different ways to measure the success of communication. The boss looks for completion of a task, the advertiser looks at the sales, a politician examines the votes, a mother notes the obedience of the child, the coach views the score, the lover measures the response, the teacher grades the test, and the pastor examines the lives of his flock.

Successful communication is more than words; it is a human interaction that has a cycle. All communication transactions cycle through the following three stages: Connect, Transmit and Respond.

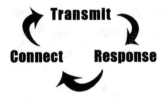

For example, if I am trying to print a document from my computer, it takes all three of the stages to get a result. This process may seem basic, but a breakdown or disconnect in communication can occur at any stage in the process.

Successful Communication

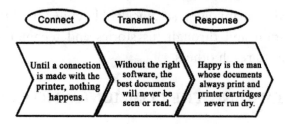

Or, if I want to order my favorite Chinese food for takeout, I call the phone number (Connect), place the order (Transmit), and then they confirm and prepare my dinner order (Respond). If I arrive at the restaurant and my order isn't ready then the reason may be one of the following:

1. Lack of Connection – The phone disconnected while placing the order, they did not understand English or I called the wrong restaurant.

2. No Transmission – They lost the order, the person taking the order didn't put it in, or the computer ate it.

3. No Response – They didn't prepare the order, my credit card was declined, or like the "Soup Nazi," they refused to serve me.

Not understanding the tri-stage nature of communication is the reason that many communication transactions are futile. Just because you talk doesn't mean that the ears or brain are engaged. Too often leaders, managers, parents or pastors assume that people will respond correctly to their instructions or requests, without making sure that a connection has been made.

Avoid the "Seaside Express"

Consider a person who spends energy writing the perfect motivational memo for the sales team. It has the perfect header, concise bullet points, the right amount of humor and a strong close. After spending most the morning writing it, he chooses the "Seaside Express" for his delivery system. He takes a copy of the memo, rolls it up, puts it into a bottle and drives down to the ocean and tosses the bottled memo into the ocean waves. He smiles with anticipation of the response of his staff.

Unfortunately, this analogy is repeated thousands of times a day. No matter how long you spend crafting a message, without a connection, delivery system or correct email address, communication failure is inevitable.

(The Seaside Express message system does have some benefit. Sometimes putting a message into a bottle and throwing it into the ocean is more productive than lecturing people who don't want to listen or are extremely critical. At times like these it is much more enjoyable to take a walk at the seashore, at least you'll get some exercise, fresh air and can enjoy the day. It's interesting to note how many times Jesus was found near the beach.)

Jesus Was a "Full Cycle" Communicator

Jesus mastered full cycle communication because he used examples that anyone and everyone had experienced. For example, Jesus coined the term, "Our Father" to describe the Almighty. This simple term and astonishing implications that it carries, was an immediate connection with his listeners. "Our Father" plugs into everyone's hopes and dreams of having a spiritual relationship that is like the one between a loving father and his children. This term transmitted a new paradigm of God who, instead of being distant and punishing, was near and interactive.

With two words Jesus redefined spirituality forever. Instead of rituals and rules, faith became alive and interactive. Jesus' term introduced Yahweh as the Heavenly Father who wants to have a relationship with the children of Adam and Eve.

The indication that communication has been successful is how people respond. Jesus always got reactions. To some, especially the children, the concept of a Heavenly Father was easy to embrace. But, for others, this concept was outrageous. Some tried to stop Jesus from communicating with threats of stoning and violence.

STAY PLUGGED IN!

If communication is like electricity then communication problems are like being unplugged or disconnected. People unplug for lots of reasons. Sometimes it is physical; they may be distracted or have hearing problems (research says that over half of your audience has hearing difficulties). People may unplug because they don't understand us or think that what we are saying is silly. Internal or emotional unplugs come from sources like fear, lies, anger, bitterness or addictions. Spiritual disconnections may come from a loss of truth and betrayal of destiny or idolatry of disappointment.

Often when we stop listening or unplug, we haven't got a clue why or know when it happens until we slow down long enough to think, listen and feel.

Effective communication is interactive and cycles through all the stages. Sometimes, even though we have done everything correctly to communicate, the anticipated response does not occur. This may or may not be the fault of the communicator. Honest communication does not manipulate, but respects the listeners and gives them the freedom to respond as they wish.

POOR HONEYBEES

When I am lost, I often refuse to look at the map and waste time driving around looking for a familiar sign. Perhaps if my internal compass was set like a honeybee or a migrating bird, there might be some hope. But recent reports tell us that the abundance of cell phone, Wi-Fi, and microwave signals that fill the atmosphere are upsetting nature. Honeybees can't find their way back to the hive and are dying because our technology has confused their internal guidance signals. We must pray that technology does not cause the same problems for us.

JESUS UNDERSTOOD HOW TO CONNECT

Communication success is difficult. Jesus was a successful communicator, but he was also very realistic. In a simple story about a farmer, he described the disappointment and challenges of everyday communication.

Once again an immense crowd gathered around Him on the beach as He was teaching, so He got into a boat and sat down and talked from there.

His usual method of teaching was to tell the people stories. One of them went like this: "Listen! A farmer decided to sow some grain. As he scattered it across his field some of it fell on a path, and the birds came and picked it off of the hard ground and ate it. Some fell on thin soil with underlying rock. It grew up quickly enough, but soon wilted beneath the hot sun and died because the roots had no nourishment in the shallow soil. Other seeds feel among thorns that shot up and crowded the young plants so that they produced no grain. But some of the seeds fell into good soil and yielded 30 times as much as he had planted – some of it even 60 or 100 times a much! If you have ears, listen!"

– Mark 4: 3–9, *The Living New Testament*

Other versions conclude with: *"He that hath ears to hear, let him hear"* or *"Are you listening to this? Really listening?"*

After Jesus told his disciples this story, they asked for an explanation. The seed represents the word and message and the situations describe the four reactions that people have to information. This parable clearly identifies the full cycle of communication with the three stages: Connect, Transmit, and Respond. The four situations show how communication can be stolen, withered, choked or successful.

"The sower sows the message. Those alongside the path where the message is sown are people who no sooner hear it than the Adversary comes and takes away the message sown in them." This first seed is an example of not having a connection with someone before you download information. The person may not be listening, or there is a bad phone signal and they never receive what is transmitted. In a work environment, some individuals who are threatened by what we are saying can snatch our seed by telling others not to listen to us and so erode our leadership.

The second seed starts to grow but then withers because there isn't any root or commitment to support the response. This is an example of an incomplete transmission, just like a person who begins a project but drops it because he doesn't have the time, resources or motivation to complete it. *"Likewise, those receiving seek on rocky patches are people who hear the message and joyfully accept it at once; but they have no root in themselves. So they hold out for a while, but as soon as some trouble or persecution arises on account of the message, they immediately fall away."*

Have you ever had to sever a partnership because the other person's values and objectives were different than yours? This is the example of the third communication seed, which grows well, but with time, is choked and trapped by weeds and thorns. The opportunity is terminated before the reward arrives. *"Others are those sown among thorns – they hear the message; but the worries of the world, the deceitful glamour of wealth and all the other kinds of desires push in and choke the message; so that it produces nothing."* – Mark 4: 14–19, *Complete Jewish Bible.*

One of the most rewarding parts of being a coach and mentor is seeing how much people can grow. *"But the one sown on the good ground – this is the one who hears and understands the word, who does bear fruit and yields: some 100, some 60, some 30 times (what was sown)"* Matthew 13: 23, *HCSB.* Fortunately, there are seeds of communication that complete the full cycle. In the Mark 4 version of the same story it says, "But the seed planted in the good earth represents those who hear the Word, embrace it, and produce a harvest beyond their wildest dreams."[10]

How does Jesus' story relate to today's communication problems? It illustrates that communication is not as easy as it looks. The late Dr. Edwin Louis Cole noted that in this story, Jesus pointed out that often the culture was the culprit and accounted for a loss of three quarters of the seed. In today's culture, the level of distraction and resistance to completed communication is as high, if not greater.[11]

[10] Pages 95–96, Mark 4:3–20, THE MESSAGE, The New Testament, Eugene H. Peterson, NavPress, Colorado Springs, CO, 1993.
[11] Dr. Edwin Louis Cole, Founder of the Christian Men's Movement, www.EdCole.org, www.EdColeLibrary.com.

It doesn't matter whether you are in the workplace, classroom or church; bosses and teachers share that they are having problems getting to events because they simply don't remember. It takes work to repeat messages or build a consistent crowd because:

- People are busy.
- People don't listen well and depend on you reminding them, like commercials.
- Younger generations make fewer commitments and respond "in the moment."

In telling the story about the Sower and seed, which is also know as Parable of the Four Soils,[12] Jesus was not discouraged by the seed that didn't make it. Instead he noted that the seeds that reached maturity more than made up for the loss of the others. It is important to focus on the people who do hear our message, respond and grow.

In the next chapter we will consider the charismatic communication of Jesus and build the foundation of communication principles. These will help us understand how to plant seeds for a productive communication harvest.

SUMMARY

We live in a media saturated, A.D.D. world. This Information Age has changed the way we live, work, play, love and relax. Media technology has created great opportunities, but also overloaded us and caused media addiction. The "Fourth Estate" Media is rapidly becoming the dominant force in shaping public opinion. In spite of the flood of media experiences, nothing can replace the impact of personal interaction and the power of word-of-mouth.

Effective communication is a cycle, which has three stages: Connect, Transmit and Respond. A communication disconnect can occur during any of these stages. Jesus was a realistic communicator who understood that the culture provided distractions that would compete for the attentions of those he was trying to reach. His focus

---

[12] This is found in Matthew 13: 3–8, Mark 4: 3–8, Luke 8: 5–8 and was explained by Jesus in a private teaching to the disciples in Matthew 13: 19–23, Mark 4: 14–20, Luke 8: 11–15. The NIV translation uses the Parable of the Four Soils instead of Parable of Sower.

was not on those he lost but on those whose response would be fruitful...and transcend his existence.

You don't have to be on stage, behind a microphone, an elected official or an award winning filmmaker to be a Master Communicator. By learning from a Master Communicator, Jesus of Nazareth, all of us can improve our communication skills and improve our communications every day, everywhere and every time.

PROFILE
A Fishing Story

The long cold night lingered. The casting of nets grew tedious. None of it yielded anything in the way of a catch for either boat. You (Simon Peter) are not in the best of moods. You have fished all night with your younger brother Andrew with nothing to show for it.

The morning's light finds you washing the nets and getting to go home for breakfast and sleep. In the distance, you see this crowd coming closer. They follow the new rabbi who has been baptizing down at the Jordan. He's been the talk of the town and has taught at the synagogue. You wonder why in the world they are down here at this time of the morning.

You are ready to pack it in and head for home. The nets are folded. And then the rabbi comes toward you and asks if he can sit on your boat and if you will push out from shore. You are honored that the rabbi makes a request, but doesn't he think it could wait till after breakfast? Still you do it, slightly curious as to what all these people find so fascinating about this guy.

So, you push out from the shore. The gentle breeze rocks the boat slightly. This rabbi starts to speak. The crowd stops pushing one another and they sit down, now able to hear these stories. The water and hills act like a natural microphone and help all to enjoy the expression and stories of this teacher.

Even though you try your best to not be impressed with this Jesus, after a few minutes you are caught up in the teaching. This is different than anything you have ever heard. No wonder the crowds and children keep asking him for one more story.

You sit listening for an hour, then another, and then you lose track of time. A moment later, the rabbi stops and turns to you and says he wants to pay you for your time. He tells you to go out into the deep water and cast your net for a catch. You can't believe your ears – is this guy crazy? Doesn't he realize that the only reason he was able to get you out in the boat was because last night's fishing trip was a zero!

You say, "Master, we have fished all night and not gotten anything."

(You try to help him realize that this is not a great idea. Even a child knows that by this time of day the fish are sleeping in the cool of the deep water. He may know teaching but he doesn't know fish like you do. Rats, you already washed the nets.)

"But at your word, I will do it!

(Gosh, you hope this is over soon. Just when you were starting to like this guy.... Everyone is looking at you and the guys are sure to give you a hard time about it.)

You motion to your brother Andrew to jump on board. He jumps and laughs, happy to have a few minutes with Yeshua. Your fishing partners, James and John ask you if you want them to come. You shake your head no, deciding that you and Andrew can handle the small, if any, catch.

The breeze quickens and catches the sail and pushes you out toward the deep. You aren't that far out and the Rabbi nods his head telling you to drop the nets. Andrew looks at you with a questioning look. You simply shrug your shoulders and give him the "whatever" look.

As you feed the nets out in a circular pattern you notice a slight rippling behind you. Minutes after the last of the net is released you feel a weight like an anchor that starts to pull the boat backward. You realize that the net is filling with a weight of fish that you have never known before. Where did these fish come from? You grab the net and start to pull and all your muscles strain from the load. You are the strongest of the group and are often able to pull the catch in without much help.

Andrew's eyes get wide and he yells to James and John on shore to join them. Will they get there in time before the fish slip out of the nets? This is the biggest catch you have ever had. Oh no, the nets are starting to rip with the weight. Will the entire catch be lost?

As the second boat pulls up they start pulling fish into the boat as quickly as possible. These fish are huge and there are so many of them. The four of you pull fish in as fast as you can. The rabbi laughs and helps to steady the boat. As James and John put their net around yours, it starts to rip with the weight of the catch also. As you pull more and more fish into the boat, the weight of the catch starts to sink the boats. Never have you seen such a catch. It is the catch of a lifetime and worth a year's wages.

As Andrew and James cry out to other boats on shore to come and help. You wonder – *Why is the favor of the Lord on you?*

Who is this rabbi? How can he command the fish in the sea? You feel ashamed and fall at his feet begging his mercy for your arrogance and pride.

As you arrive at shore, the remaining crowd has gathered around. The women and servants looking for fish come with coins in hand. Children run to town to tell others about the great catch. The beach becomes a

How much fish did Peter catch?

Fishing was a major part of the Galilean economy and lifestyle. Peter would have caught tilapia, carp and sardines. These were sold, dried or made into fish sauce that was imported through the Mediterranean world.

We don't know how large Peter's boat was, but in 1986 a fishing boat of the time was discovered. It was 26.5 feet long, 7.5 feet wide and 4.5 feet deep. It could hold one ton—five crewmembers and the catch or ten people. If Peter and his partners had boats of this size and the nets were breaking, then it means the catch could have been one or two tons or more.[13]

---

[13] Page. 1676, *Archaeological Study Bible*, Fishing in New Testament Times, Zondervan, Grand Rapids, MI, 2005.

marketplace filled with laughter and joy. As the last of the fish are carried off to the shops and drying trays, you feel too exhausted to even count all the coins in your bag.

The Rabbi has been watching with a secret smile on his face. As he turns to walk away, he says to the four of you, "Follow me and I will make you fishers of men."

Fishers of men. What can he mean? But from the weight of the catch and wealth of the day, you decide to follow Yeshua.

CHAPTER 4
STORIES – CASTING THE NET

All the world's a stage and the men and women on it merely players.
– William Shakespeare

STORIES – THE FIRST STEP

Jesus was a Master Storyteller whose artistry and truth reflected like a mirror and guided like a compass. Stories are the most recognized communication tool of Jesus and the first step of the S.I.M.P.L.E.™ Method. This chapter explains the importance and impact of stories and evaluates the ways Jesus used parables, images and metaphors to reach out, position, protect and to build relationships. In a media saturated world, stories are a key to effective and meaningful communication.

LOVE OF STORIES

In the fifth grade I became bored with recess, not that I wasn't popular or a successful dodge ball player. But instead of running around on the blacktop after lunch, I asked my teacher to let me go to the first grade class and read them stories. She agreed and once or twice a week I would carry a favorite story book down to read to the attentive little ones. The night before, I "test marketed" these tales on my younger brother and sisters to make sure they'd be a hit. Was it the Arbitron diary or the natural television instincts that caused me to understand the importance of research at age nine?

Recalling those times, I envision the scene from the back of the old classroom, with sunshine streaming through what seemed to be eternally tall brick framed windows. As I stood outside the classroom door, the teacher turned off the lights to silence the group. Being theatrical, I relished the moment, and tiptoed across the linoleum as the excited twitter began. The eager six-year-olds, some with arms outstretched over pine veneer desktops, gazed with expectation as I held up each new picture. A hush ruled the room as I patiently panned each book illustration in its time so all could see. The hands on the clock seemed to slow down magically as we shared these classic stories and fables of old.

When the ending was read, after a collective sigh, the predictable pleading began, "Can we have one more story?" This familiar request has been heard around the world since families everywhere sat down together over a good book or family legend.

THE MAGIC OF ONCE UPON A TIME

Like leaping onto a magical carpet or riding on the back of the North Wind, the words – "Once upon a time" – make us feel tingly with expectation. Once upon a time…and so the story begins. These simple words cause the youngest to listen and wisest to pause. As adults, our stories begin with phrases such as:

"Tonight we begin our newscast with a visit to…. "

"Like sand through the hourglass so go the days of our lives…. "

"In a galaxy far, far away…. "

THE POWER OF STORIES

Why do some stories touch us so quickly and so deeply? How do they grab us? Why is it so hard to put that special book down or turn off that movie, even though we have seen it a dozen times? Psychologists and psychiatrists will tell you many scientific reasons that stories work, but in simple terms, stories work because they can touch us on so many levels.

Stories teach, inspire, direct, correct, entertain and change us. Why? Is it because they open a new door and take us on an instant journey?

Stories touch our minds and woo our hearts. They stimulate our senses and help us to see ourselves in the lives, loves, struggles and victories of others.

Stories are a conduit for learning. They instruct us and help us to gather information easily. Stories are like presents that we can't wait to open.

Stories provide a safe place to visit where no one can hurt you. You are free to experience without a fear of failure or sense of deficiency. Stories make us laugh, cry and become a part of us.

Within the freedom of a story you can do anything, go anywhere, try everything without buying a ticket. The only cost is time.

THE MASTER STORYTELLER

Jesus was a master storyteller and crafter of parables, word pictures, analogies, and visual imagery. Even though the stories Jesus told may have seemed childish to critics, their depth and spirit made them timeless and powerful. Like a stealth missile, they flew under the radar screen of the educated and detonated within the spirits of multitudes. The educated laughed, the religious scoffed, yet the common people loved them for their relevancy. But even with their simplicity, Jesus told stories that had multiple levels and hidden meanings. Only those closest to him or the openhearted could appreciate their value.

When Did Jesus Use Stories?

Jesus used stories all the time and in every communication situation, public or private, from the rich to the poor and the religious to the worldly. He used them in small groups and one-on-one. Jesus used them to address massive crowds with great ethnic variety. The gospels explain that Jesus always addressed large crowds with parables, and *"without a parable He did not speak to them."* – Matthew 13: 34, King James (KJ)

How Often Did Jesus Use Stories and Word Pictures?

Jesus used stories more than any other spiritual leader. In evaluating the gospels, it shows that almost 35% of the recorded words of Jesus included a story, parable, word picture, allegory, simile or metaphor. There are over fifty-one different stories and parables in the combined texts of the gospels. Stories were a foundational and critical part of every message, teaching and interaction. The stories Jesus told have been considered artistic. Regardless of your opinion on that, these simple stories have power.

How Did Jesus Use Stories?

Jesus used stories as tools, shields and bridges. He used them to teach, preach, explain, protect, rebuke, defend and relate. Jesus used them offensively to reach out to the world and express his message. He uses them defensively to protect himself, his motives and his dreams. He used them to build community, intimacy and to help others climb heaven's ladder.

Living Stories and Active Sayings

In fact, 2,000 years later and around the globe, you could say that Jesus' words live on. Every day his stories are read, told, taught, studied and analyzed by millions. These words remain active and part of social interaction. Most Westerners can easily recognize them. Jesus' sayings and stories are so ingrained that they are part of everyday conversation and they are standard cultural references. For example, do you know what the following comments mean?

No one can serve two masters. (That person is trying to do two things at once and may have divided loyalties. It describes a person who may need to focus. Or this could be a person who is selling out or conflicted by two opportunities, which may oppose each other.)

Don't throw your pearls before swine. (Don't waste your valuable time, information or resources on people who don't appreciate it.)

The wise man builds his house upon the rock. (Yes, that is part of a commercial, but Jesus said that the foundation of our lives is critical. We all need a solid foundation.)

They need to separate the sheep from the goats. (This office or committee has some people who do not fit. There may be a need to separate out or fire those who aren't team players – who are stubborn, misfits or disloyal – and not willing to follow the lead of the manager.)

Jesus used stories everyday, everywhere and with everyone. What was the result? These stories and their messages have had universal impact and are still with us today. This is nothing less than remarkable. Jesus was a master storyteller whose teachings and communications have stood the test of time.

APPLICATION

Use more stories, especially short ones! Jesus used stories, word pictures, analogies and images almost 40% of the time and in every type of communication situation. If you are communicating to a large audience through television or a public speaking venue, it is critical that you use stories and examples in your message. Jesus did not speak without them, neither should we!

COMMUNION OF STORYTELLING

Communion and community occur when stories are told. If you have worked outside of major cities, you know that telling stories is part of the culture and part of doing business. Some of my favorite times in Texas have been in coffee shops listening to the great stories that the farmers, ranchers and oilmen shared. If you wanted to do business with these guys, you had to learn to listen as they spun their yarns.

Jesus conducted most of his ministry in the countryside. Were small town people better listeners or did they have more time to listen? It is interesting that all of his disciples, except for Judas, came from the rural Galilee area by the sea. Compared to the sophisticated inhabitants of Jerusalem, they were considered "country folks" with a more humble social status.

In the news business, a friend of mine was considered the "Bard of Television News," Don Fitzpatrick. Of Irish descent, we all loved to hear Fitz tell his stories and chart the career path of any major anchor or television reporter. While writing this book, I learned he passed away. Like many others, I miss his legendary yarns. The same sweet longing fills me when I think of losing friends like Don or family like my grandfather. I miss them and wish I could hear their heart-warming stories one more time. Stories are the glue that binds people together. Regardless of culture, stories and word pictures weave individuals together.

STORYTELLER DOLLS

Have you ever seen a pottery Storyteller doll from the Pueblo Indian artists? These charming pottery statues are of a seated adult Indian (usually a woman) who is holding and surrounded by many children. There are sometimes a dozen miniature children looking up at the elder woman who has her mouth open in a singing position.

While showing me several of these unique pieces of pottery, my dear friend Anne Barge told me their origin. The storyteller images represent what was an essential part of tribal life for the Pueblos. During the day the parents would leave the village to hunt or work the fields and leave the children behind with the grandparents. The grandparents gathered the kids and sang stories to them. These songs and stories were based on tribal knowledge, education, identity – their past and their future.

The storytellers are the quintessential image of the power of stories. Looking at these simple yet beautiful pottery storytellers, reminds us that all the tribes of the earth are built with stories.

APPLICATION

Stories are the universal building tool of culture. Stories connect us to our identity, our families, our tribe, and our ethnic backgrounds and to our country. By learning tales about others we learn who we are.

STORIES AND THE EASTERN CULTURE

In Jesus' day, stories were the coin of communication and an integral part of life. Memorization of large portions of Scripture and wisdom literature was part of every boy's education. The law and stories were the common reference points. It is important to remember that Jesus lived and succeeded within the culture of his time. To best understand how he communicated, it is important to look at his stories and images through the glasses of his culture rather than those of our modern, Western world.[14]

Let's revisit the "separate the sheep from the goats" reference. Jesus' audience, especially the religious teachers, knew immediately what this example meant and its implications. Sheep will follow the voice of the shepherd and are much easier to manage because they can be herded. Goats are very independent, stubborn and like to choose their own path whether safe or unsafe. The very nature of the animals demonstrated their value.

By using this analogy, Jesus explained that the entrance to heaven would be like a shepherd separating the sheep from the goats. The faithful and kind would be let into heaven and the unloving and proud would be rejected.

Every culture is unique but there is a basic difference between the Western (American and European) and Eastern (Middle-East, Asian) cultures. Westerners think in a "Greek" or analytical thought process based on man's logic and experiences. The Eastern culture thinks in a mystic mind set which deals with images and stories. Another way to think of it is: Westerners are very left-brained and Easterners are more right-brained.

The way different cultures view problems and solutions is very interesting.

For example, if I asked you when does spring begin? A Westerner would tell me the date, time, equinox or almanac information. A person with the Eastern mindset would say when the birds start to build their nest or when the moon is full.

Jesus lived in a time, in a society and in a culture in which oral tradition was an integral part of existence. To appreciate and understand the meaning of Jesus' stories and analogies, it is important to place them in context of the Jewish and Mediterranean cultures of the 1st century A.D.

[14] Vanderlaan, Ray, www.FollowtheRabbi.com. His articles and DVD series are extremely informative and provide excellent research on what life was like in Jesus' time.

THE ORIGINAL "BIG FISH" STORY

One of the first "promises" that Jesus made to four young men on the shores of Galilee, was, "Come with me and I will make you a fisher of men." The verb for fish implies to catch alive, not to kill (which is a good thing because catching those dead ones is difficult). As the previous profile described, Simon (later called Peter) and his younger brother Andrew, along with their fishing partners James and John, had a life-changing encounter with Jesus. After a long and fruitless night of fishing, followed by a double-header sermon, Jesus asked Simon Peter to push out into the deeper water and let his nets down for a catch.

The fisherman told Jesus, in polite terms, that was a waste of time. But out of respect for the rabbi, Simon Peter did what he was told. They were shocked when the nets filled with the catch of a lifetime. Simon called for backup and everyone had enough cash to set aside for retirement. Realizing his foolishness, Simon fell down in front of Jesus asking him to forgive him for being such a turkey.

After the catch was gathered, it was then that Jesus told the four young men to follow him and "I will make you fishers of men."

When the miracle of the fish occurred differs between John and the other gospels. John tells a similar story that happens after the resurrection of Christ. (John. 21:1–14) But tells that they met him while following John the Baptist. In Luke's gospel (Luke 4:38–39) Jesus had healed Simon's mother of a fever before-hand. Regardless, Jesus made good on his promise and taught them all how to be "Fishers of Men."

APPLICATION

Jesus used terms to which individuals could relate. Fishing to fishermen, planting to farmers, sheep to shepherds. It is important to use images that people can relate to on multiple levels – experiences, emotions, etc.

Prepare and choose stories and examples that are culturally relevant to the group with which you are communicating. There is nothing more embarrassing than to get 2,000 blank looks when you mention a character in a Jane Austen novel to a group of pre-teens. Mention Raven and they can even recite the last ten outfits that she wore on her Disney show.

WHY DO STORIES WORK? USE THE BASKET

To explain how stories function, imagine that you are on a game show and the objective is to catch as many balls as possible. But you only get paid for the ones you can hold onto.

The bell rings and one by one, faster and faster, all sorts of balls are thrown at you – golf balls, tennis balls, soft balls, soccer and footballs come whizzing across the room. How many balls can you catch before you start dropping them? Maybe four or five if they are small and you use your pockets, but how many can you hold and catch when they are large? After your hands and arms are full, it doesn't take long before there is a stream of missed balls bouncing all over the room, and you are frustrated because of so much missed opportunity.

Now imagine that you get another chance at the game but this time you are given a large basket or mesh bag that you can use to store the balls that you get. How many balls can you catch and hold now? How much more money do you win?

It is important to remember that this analogy is the way most people deal with information and facts. This is the same way we throw words, facts and information at people, at different speeds, directions and intensities. But, when we tell a story it gives context and makes a virtual net or basket so that people can catch, remember, retain and access more information.

In the Information Age Stories Are Critical tools

Today's media culture includes more stories and visual images than ever before. This makes the telling and the using of them even more critical. Unfortunately, many people don't realize how much the rules for communication success have changed.

Have you ever tried to find something in your computer hard drive that was mislabeled? Thank heavens for the search function. Without it many of us would never find those files with that critical information. In computer terms, stories create files in our minds files so that we can categorize, sort and retrieve information quickly.

One of the major problems that people make in mass communication is trying to impart multiple facts without context, or without the mental basket provided by the story. This means that instead of being mentally filed, the information goes into the "Spam file" and the brain hits the delete button. Even though the boss's information was valuable, without the context provided by the story, the communication exchange is rendered useless.

Application

Providing stories as information files are critical tools in a data-flooded world. Stories, visual images and analogies help people to remember information because it gives the mind something to grasp, to file and to store. Like using a file or a basket, framing information within the context of a story helps our brain to place the information so it can be accessed more quickly. It helps us store the info so it avoids the instant trashcan.

Men Fishers

Let's return to the fishing analogy. In Jesus' time fishermen used lines, spears and nets. This fishing gear can be compared to the way Jesus used stories, parables, allegories, metaphors, similes and analogies. He used this picturesque way of communicating which drew the listener closer to him and clarified his message.

Parables are simple short stories about everyday objects and experiences that teach a moral or spiritual lesson. Analogies are stories with hidden meaning. He used both. Examples of his parables are: "The Prodigal Son," "The Good Samaritan" and "The Sower and the seed." Any of these could easily begin with "Once upon a time."

Some define a parable as an "earthly story with a heavenly meaning." This book underscores that explanation. Scholars separate these stories into the categories of parables, exemplary stories, allegories, and his use of figures of speech, such as simile. Jesus used mental imagery through his use of simile, metaphor and analogy. His use of stories and way he talked, cast a net that drew in his audience. When Jesus spoke it was like getting a double-chocolate chunk cookie right out of a warm oven.

The dynamic part of his stories and word pictures is the way they have both literal and figurative meaning. For example: Why is a seed like truth? Why is a shepherd like a leader? Why is the spirit like the wind? Why did the Almighty call his word a lamp?

Often Jesus' stories and figures of speech compare a spiritual principle to a common experience. He used similes in phrases or sentences. For example: the Kingdom of God is like a shepherd who went to find his lost sheep. Because of his use of the language, complex concepts immediately crystallize into ideas as simple as a cup of coffee on the breakfast table.

APPLICATION

Jesus used stories and ideas that painted word pictures, which drew his audience in like a fish on a line. His teaching included full stories, word pictures, similes, and metaphors as well as other verbal images. Using the language the way he did will strengthen speeches. It will increase the impact of our conversations and make all of our interactions more memorable.

PARABLES ARE EVERYWHERE

PARABLE – DEFINED PURPOSE

If asked what a parable is, most people will tell you that it is a nice story with a moral. The word parable has become such a common term that the real function and meaning of these stories has been forgotten. The word "parable" means, "laying by the side of" or "a casting alongside." The root "Para" is the same for the words parallel (like railroad tracks) and paragraph (lay aside thoughts). The back half of the word comes from the Greek verb "ballo" which means to throw, to scatter, cast into, to pour out or to insert.

How interesting that the action involved in this word is the same action that a fisherman uses to cast his net, a sower casts the seed, and a warrior throws a spear. This means that there are two parts of the function of a parable:

• The first intent of a parable is to come along side a person's experiences and through stories or images offer people information, insights or revelations.

• The second function of a parable is to throw, cast, pour and insert information into those who are listening. Like pouring water into a bottle but using a funnel, parables help you to insert information into people more easily.

This reinforces the previous principle that communication is three parts – connecting, transmitting and response. Advertisers measure the success of their ads through sales. Teachers measure with tests. God measures lives with actions. So connecting alone isn't enough. The connection and the transmission are to bring about a result.

The function of a parable is to impart information through relevant stories. Master Communicators know how to use parables for maximum impact. A parable is more than a nice story; it is made to transmit and change.

PARABLES TODAY

So where do we find parables today? Everywhere! They just have different names such as commercials, pop-ups, news stories, soap operas, movies, songs, print ads or novels. If ever there was a Communications Matrix it is now. Movies are often allegories with classic plot lines and messiah figures that echo the timeless stories that we love and celebrate.

Jesus had great success in his storytelling and here are some of the rules he followed:

1. THE STORY LINES WERE SIMPLE AND OFTEN ABOUT CAUSE AND EFFECT

For example:
- A sower sows the seed and some plants grow and others do not.
- The king has a banquet and invites the poor because the rich were too busy.
- The slave is not forgiving to others as the master is to him so he gets payback.
- A crime victim is refused by two "righteous" men and taken care of by a lowlife.
- The wayward son squanders his inheritance and returns home repentant.

The simplicity of Jesus' stories helps focus attention on deeper truth. Great storytellers such as Mark Twain, Will Rodgers, Edward Murrow, George Lucas, and others know the power of simplicity.

Garrison Keillor is one of America's favorite storytellers on the weekly radio show, *Prairie Home Companion*. In addition to having a wonderful voice and presentation style, Keillor tells fictional stories about everyday life in Lake Woebegone, Minnesota. The stories are about ordinary activities told in an extraordinary way. When Keillor speaks, I find myself hanging on every word and chuckling continually. The brevity of his stories reminds us that – the unspoken is what activates what we see in our minds, which in turn makes stories, even more enthralling.

They say such nice things about people at their funeral that it makes me sad to realize that I'm going to miss mine by just a few days.
– Garrison Keillor

APPLICATION

Parables did not contain unnecessary facts and details. When you use stories remember that less is more. In crisis or adversarial situations, using fewer words helps to guarantee that your message will be heard with the intent in which it was given. Fewer words protect you from being misquoted and misunderstood.

The one who welcomes you welcomes Me, and the one who welcomes Me welcomes Him who sent Me. And whoever gives just one cup of cold water to one of these little ones because he is a disciple – I assure you: He will never lose his reward!" – Jesus, Matthew 10: 40,42, *HCSB*.

2. PARABLES USED THE ORDINARY AND FAMILIAR.

All of the parables Jesus told had familiar experiences, objects and issues. He taught with the elements around him. When sitting in fields filled with flowers he talked about the lilies and birds. By the sea, he spoke about fishing. On the hills where the sheep grazed, he talked about shepherds. Jesus told stories about planting, baking, working, ungrateful servants, losing coins, and seeds. He introduced a familiar topic but gave it a new meaning.

Using familiar objects makes the story and the message even more memorable. In the future, when a person encounters the same experience or objects, he will be reminded of the story and the information in the same way hearing a familiar tune evokes memories.

But here is bread that comes down from heaven, which a man may eat and not die. I am the living bread that came down from heaven. If anyone eats of this bread, he will live forever. This bread is my flesh, which I will give for the life of the world.
– Jesus, John 6: 50–51, *NIV*

APPLICATION

Use familiar objects and experiences to create stories for the audience. This is a matter of knowing your audience and developing age and/or job appropriate material for them. People bond when common ground is traversed through stories. Use popular movies; television characters, headlines, current water cooler topics and the news buzz to build your content.

3. PARABLES ADDRESSED A SPECIFIC ISSUE AND OFTEN HAD AN UNEXPECTED TWIST

One day a Religious Scholar asked Jesus a clever question, "Who is my neighbor?" In response, Jesus told an unforgettable story with an unexpected hero.

The story tells of a man traveling the rugged, dangerous road from Jerusalem to Jericho. Along the way, robbers attacked him. He was beaten and left half dead by the side of the road. A priest came along but crossed over to the other side of the road and walked right by. A Levite came along and did the same. Then a Samaritan walked up. He picked up the injured man, bandaged his wounds and took him to an inn to be looked after. He paid the innkeeper the equivalent of two days wages and promised to reimburse him for additional expenses. *Jesus then asked the scholar, which of the three men was the man's neighbor? The young man responded that the one who dealt kindly to him. Jesus then told him to, "Go and do the same."* – Luke 10: 25–37, HCSB.

With the famous parable of the "Good Samaritan," Jesus stretches his listener's minds. The religious expert asked the question, thinking his beliefs and behaviors would be reaffirmed. Instead Jesus strips away the self-righteousness, pride and prejudice by forcing people to look at the truth of their actions rather than their social status.

In Jewish culture, choosing a Samaritan as a hero was a real stretch. The culture was highly prejudicial and class controlled. A Samaritan was considered to be inferior in all ways. Yet, in the story he demonstrates the true nature of brotherly love. The priest and the Levite, who were supposed to be the standard for righteousness, proved to be shallow and cold hearted. With this story Jesus created a mirror, which forced his listeners to examine their own hearts and actions.

It is interesting to note that Jesus did not judge the characters within his stories. Instead he let the listeners make their own judgments and ask questions of them. Am I a good neighbor? Do my actions match my beliefs? Do I live my truth? Telling stories that raise personal questions, allows the message to be internalized. The story is not meant to become the focus of debates, but rather to make the listener think.

Sometimes the unexpected element in Jesus' parables incorporated exaggeration to make a point. In "the Prodigal Son," the father not only welcomes the son home but also celebrates his return with a feast. In the parable of the "Unforgiving Servant," the master forgives a debt of over $10 million dollars, which was an unbelievable sum in those days. But the one who was forgiven refused to do the same with a small debt owed to him.

APPLICATION

Stories can be a mirror, which allows people to see themselves, their actions and their motives more clearly. Jesus used the elements of surprise, exaggeration and unlikely heroes to make his points.

4. JESUS DID NOT ALWAYS EXPLAIN HIS STORIES TO THE CROWDS

Jesus' stories were not your typical story with a punch line. He wasn't looking for the quick laugh that tickled the ears and filled the offering plate. Jesus' told stories that got inside the listener's head and made people think. He would often tell parables without explaining their meanings. Later, when he was with the disciples, he would teach and explain the meaning of the stories.

The disciples didn't understand and asked "why?" Jesus often answered with what sounded like a riddle. Even his answers left something for them to figure out. Jesus told them that the secrets of heaven were for not for those who would listen but not understand, look and not perceive, or whose hearts were hard (Isaiah 6: 9–11).

Jesus wasn't looking for an immediate reaction or for popularity. He plowed the ground of men's hearts and minds for deeper understanding. Superficial teaching is like junk food that lacks nutritional value. Jesus knew that people have to work for real answers to questions. He understood that being smart or knowledgeable does not promise wisdom or compassion. It was like – "This is for me to know and you to search out!"

Now we can learn from the master and use stories to cast nets. The stories can include familiar experiences used to bring understanding, truth or information. When ideas or seeds are planted, some grow. Some don't. Jesus never felt pressured by or responsible for the growth of others. He challenged his audience continually with the words, "He who has ears to hear let him listen."

APPLICATION

A little mystery can be a good thing. When using stories it is not always necessary to fully explain them to the audience. Remember people are responsible for their own growth and change comes from within. It is important to encourage people to listen and to highlight and repeat key information that they need to remember.

When the temple police came to the chief priest and Pharisees, who asked them, "Why haven't you brought him?"

The police answer, "No man ever spoke like this!"

– John 7: 45–46, *HCSB*

5. JESUS USED STORIES DEFENSIVELY TO DEFLECT HIS CRITICS AND PROTECT HIS MESSAGE

There is nothing more threatening to a leader than the popularity of the new guy in town. The religious leaders, experts, scribes, politicians and priests of his time all tried to find ways to entrap Jesus. They used their best questions and theological issues to set him up. But time after time, he blew them away with the simplicity and logic of his answers. Like a skilled swordsman, sometimes he deflected the blow and other times he countered with a direct hit.

Here is an example of how he used stories and analogies to deflect an attack. At a winter festival the Jewish leaders surrounded him in the temple and said, "Tell us plainly who you are. Are you the Messiah?" Jesus replied, saying that sheep listen to the voice of the good shepherd. He told them that he had answered the question, but they couldn't hear him because they were not his sheep and they didn't know his voice. He answered their question with a well-known analogy that protected him and his role.

The leaders grew angry at his reply. But Jesus knew there are times for "vision casting" and times for "protecting the vision." It takes discernment to know the difference and wisdom to know what to do. That is why preparation and rehearsal are important tools in difficult communication situations.

USE A MIRROR

One of the important defensive moves that fighters use in hand-to-hand combat is to leverage the weight of the opponent against him. This is what Jesus did when the religious leaders criticized him. Jesus used parables that like a mirror reflected the truth of their actions back at them. One time the leaders, jealous of his popularity and miracles, challenged his right to teach in the temple. Jesus told a parable that reflected the weight of their beliefs.

The story was about two sons whose father asked them to go work in the vineyard. The first son said no but then changed his mind and went to work. The second son said yes but then didn't go. Jesus asked, "Which son did what the father wanted?" The reply was the first.

This story showed that actions not words were the true measure of obedience. Jesus showed that the actions of a person's life, not showy ceremonies or pious activities were important.

Jesus used dozens of parables to protect and defend the truth of his actions. These analogies were direct and offensive. For example, Jesus called some of his critics, blind guides, fruitless trees and open graves. These aren't the most politically sensitive terms that I would have used. But they worked. In the chapters on Interaction and Multi-track communication techniques, we will examine how Jesus disarmed his opponents in greater detail.

APPLICATION

Parables and analogies can be used to defuse, deflect and protect against criticism and verbal attack. Sometimes Jesus used parables like a mirror to reflect the truth of their motives. Other times he used analogies to confuse his opponents and shield his mission.

It is important to be prepared with stories and parables, both short and long when dealing with opposition and debates. This is more than "spin" and positioning. It is finding specific examples and analogies that explain or protect your position or company. Parables like these are the quickest way to unseat your critics and gain the respect and hopefully support of the audience.

WHO WILL TELL YOUR STORY?

The importance of stories is more than the transmission of information. Stories are the coinage of what each person leaves behind in the lives of others. For some they will construct a legacy of buildings while others leave the gentle stories of baked cookies and summer gardens. We all have stories that we want to leave with others.

The importance of personal stories is beautifully and violently communicated in the movie *Windtalker*. This film is about how Navaho Indians were drafted in World War II to be the radio operators or code talkers for infantry. All of the previous codes used by the Army had been broken by the Japanese, except for the Navaho language. Protecting the code was paramount and officers were instructed to kill the Navaho radio operators rather than let them be captured by the Japanese. In the movie Nicholas Cage plays a hardened officer who is assigned to "protect" his code talker. The Navaho solider attempts to form a relationship with Cage's character but he is rejected continually.

At a critical moment in the movie, the Navaho confronts Cage with, "Who will tell your story when you die?" Cage's character sees the dust of his life and the barbed wire anger that has held it into place. He has rejected love, friends, life, God and his own heart. He sees that he has become as ugly as that which he hates.

Who will tell your story? Will anyone face the rising sun and sing the song of your life. Will they give honor to your memory around the campfire?

These thoughts of light quickly dispel the ghosts that have driven Cage's character. He is renewed in the midst of hell on earth. In a critical battle, he saves the life of the Navaho who saved his spirit. The final scene of the movie transports us to an incredible vista from the top of a Southwestern plateau. The majestic walls of ancient canyons surround the Navaho solider, his wife and a young son. As the sun sets, he sings in his native language and cradles dog tags in his hand. He looks his son in the eyes and says, "Let me tell you a story of my friend, Joe. He was a brave warrior and a good friend."

Why do stories like this touch us so? Why do our hearts swell and our eyes tear up. Beyond the frail details of these stories there is universal truth that touches us all. Stories are the maps, which tell the journey of human existence.

Summary

Stories contain the substance of our lives. They are universal connectors and give us our identity, tribe and truth. Stories help us escape into another dimension where we can walk without pain, learn without fear, experience without debt and love without chains. Stories not only entertain us, but they can be like missiles that carry information into our hearts, minds and lives. Like a rare collection of bottles positioned beautifully on a shelf, stories come in different shapes, sizes and purposes.

Jesus was a Master Storyteller. He used stories to open hearts, blind eyes, prison doors and the gates of heaven. He used stories to teach and guide. When Jesus used parables, he used people's personal experiences to plant seeds of life. Jesus used his stories like nets to capture imaginations and pull the listeners into waves of understanding. In times of conflict, Jesus used stories to defend and protect the truth.

If I were to pour gold dust into your hands, what would happen? How much could you hold before it fell to the ground? Or would you ask me to give you something to hold and contain the gift? When using parables and stories in our communication, it is like giving people a beautiful box to hold the treasures that we share with them.

CHAPTER 5
INTERACTION – USING HOOKS AND BAIT

Interaction is the second principle of the S.I.M.P.L.E.™ Method of Jesus' communication techniques. Interaction is like a baited hook. It attracts attention, engages, "hooks" and draws people into the message that is being communicated. Interaction begins with the use of questions, word pictures, sound bites, riddles and props. Great interaction is like "word salt" because it flavors information and makes it taste more palatable and more memorable. Additionally, interactive tools can be used in a defensive manner to evaluate, protect and qualify the audience.

"Such is the vanity of mankind that minding what others say is a much surer way of pleasing them than talking well ourselves."
– Benjamin Franklin, *On Conversation*

FATHER OF THE AMERICAN SOUND BITE

Benjamin Franklin was a printer, inventor, scientist, politician and statesman who shaped history through his vision, wisdom, diligence and communications skills. As the "Father of the American Sound Bite" Franklin knew how to hook or engage men's minds and hearts, and how to unify their actions. Franklin began as a printer, but his talent for writing, commentary and common sense launched him into the public arena. People wanted to hear what he had to say. His ability to turn a phrase motivated the colonists and enraged the British.

If anyone knew how to make the public react it was Ben Franklin. In his early life he touched the masses with Poor Richard's Almanac. Franklin was known for sayings like:

"No gains without pains.... Eat to live, and not live to eat.... He that lies down with dogs shall rise up with fleas.... A good example is the best sermon.... Haste makes waste.... Genius without education is like silver in the mine.... Fish and visitors stink in three days.... If you want to know the value of money, try to borrow some."

Later in life, Franklin took the same common sense – wrapped in charm – to engage and connect leaders on both sides of the Atlantic. Franklin is considered "America's first great publicist." He continually reinvented both himself and the American image. "In the process, he carefully crafted his own persona, portrayed it in public, and polished it for posterity.... As an old diplomat in France, he wore a fur cap to portray the role of backwoods sage."[15]

Franklin understood the power of questions. As a politician and statesman, Franklin mastered the use of questions, humor and wit to win debates and to unite opponents. In his writings, Franklin acknowledged that his method of communicating with people changed as he matured. He discovered that rather than confronting and spending time arguing, he wrote that it was better to ask people questions and let their own answers expose their error.

Benjamin Franklin's writings, careers and accomplishments clearly illustrate the communication value of interactive tools. Franklin used memorable phrases, props, and questions to hook, capture, bridle and guide his audience. Franklin gleaned ideas for these sayings from well-known sources for his day, including the Bible, fables and classic literature. His genius was demonstrated in the gleaning. Franklin picked simple seeds of truth, dipped them in humor and seasoned them with common sense to unify the thirteen colonies. His questions turned dreams into decisions that, like gunpowder, ignited destiny. Franklin helped launch the harvest of change that birthed America and established the freedoms enjoyed today.

[15] Page 2. Walter Isaacson, *Benjamin Franklin, An American Life*, Simon and Schuster, New York, N.Y, 2003.

INTERACTION DEFINED

Interaction is the next step in building dynamic presentations. All great teachers, speakers, advertisers and web designers use interaction and interactive techniques. Stories are the foundation of the message. Interaction is what attracts them to the message. Interaction reaches out to engage the audience. Just like the flower has a scent and a peacock has feathers, interaction is the bait and hook that reaches out and pulls people into the message.

Great interactive examples are everywhere. Interactive communication is like the sidewalk and the door leading into the house. Interaction draws us inside. Master Communicators know how to use these techniques to actively involve the audience. Interaction is like "word salt" because it spices up information and makes it memorable. Interaction in the form of questions can be like a shield to protect our time and our energies.

In everyday communication, "hooks" are used to attract and draw people in. Hooks are as subtle as a newspaper headline or as grotesque as a burlesque billboard. Everyday, everywhere, we encounter and process thousands of "Interactive" messages. They are called commercials, ads, headlines, pictures, sound bites, junk mail and teases. They come in all sizes and lengths from a thirty second commercial to a five-second "stinger," like "Coming Up Next." Try though we may to block the pop-ups and delete them, they still make us want a latte or a new car. They still steal our time with questions like: "Want to know how to find that dream job?" "Looking for Mr. Right?" "Win a Free Laptop!" or "You Won – Click Now!"

Interaction means to create action, movement or exchange among or between people. Even though a simple conversation is an interaction, for a Master Communicator, "Interaction" is like a term used to describe the presentation techniques that connect and engage listeners. Sometimes interaction is used to pull you in. It helps people remember, respond and "hum along with the jingle."

Interaction helps people to engage so information can be transmitted. Just like in a TV show where the authorities are trying to trace the call placed by the killers, you have to keep them on the line long enough to get the trace. Verbal hooks and interesting sound bites help to engage people's attention and keep them with you much longer.

Interactive techniques can also be used in a defensive manner. Questions can also be used to qualify, filter and protect a person. For example, a gatekeeper, or scheduler is one of the most valuable employees of any businessperson. Screening the phone calls and meeting requests helps increase workplace effectiveness.

BACK TO FISHING

Some fish are caught with nets, while others are line-caught with a baited hook or lure. The bait attracts the fish and after they have taken a bite, the hook snags them. To catch a certain type of fish requires different lures and bait. The purpose is to attract the right fish and push away fish that are too small or the wrong kind. Sometimes we catch the wrong type of fish or turtle and reel them in only to release the hook from their mouth. This scenario illustrates the four functions of interactive techniques: Bait, Hook, Pushback, Catch and Release. Each of these will be addressed as part of the interactive process.

INTERACTION "TOOL BELT"

In the Information Age, the "Net" is a virtual matrix or web that is continually growing and developing more hooks and ways to capture our time, attention and dollars. Think of how many pop-ups, click-through and registrations you encounter during a short surf on the Internet.

A story is like a net that interests us but the interactive messages help to draw us in, hook our memory and then establish a new file in our minds. As every politician or pastor knows, it is important for people to remember what you said.

Here are the interactive tools for your tool belt.

WORD PICTURES AND SOUND BITES

Word pictures create a visual with words that help explain, frame or illustrate a point. They are short memorable phrases that make the complex easy to understand. These are brief and can be contained within a longer story or parable. In modern terms think: "Wild Thing," or "The Real Thing." Jesus' examples: Bread of Life, Born Again, Light of the World and Drink of Living Water.

In the news world, sound bites are memorable statements that establish a position, opinion or fact. Both techniques help hook the audience for the short and for the long term. Two of Jesus' sayings are: "I am the Good Shepherd," and "Who is my brother?" More modern examples are: "We try harder" and "You deserve a break today."

PROPS

Verbal props are used as visual analogies, parables, or examples. The more ordinary the prop is, the more profound the impact. It is highly probable that Jesus used the props and his locations to shape his messages. He used flowers, grapes, sheep, water, bread, and wine – all things familiar to his audience. Props are important because they stimulate both sides of the brain and become a long-term mental hook.

QUESTIONS – SEEK, FIND AND KNOTS

As discussed earlier, the Hebrew and Middle-Eastern cultures depend on questions for educational and social exchange. Jesus lived in a culture, which used questions for teaching, working, selling and praying. He was a genius in using questions for both offensive and defensive means. He used questions within the parables and after them to teach, to make people think, and to shutdown his adversaries.

RIDDLES

Riddles are statements and questions, which are like little mysteries. In Jesus' case, he used riddles to challenge people's thoughts and then refused to answer them. Riddles can act like a small bomb that blasts away rigid mindsets and traditions with a few simple ideas. This method makes people think, discuss and hopefully discover the meaning of the riddle.

QUESTIONS JESUS ASKED

Like a good rabbi, Jesus used interactive questions to open minds and to build interest. He also used questions to test receptivity, to qualify and to investigate people's motives. But even as a child, Jesus showed a remarkable talent for asking questions that amazed even the "best of the best" in Jerusalem.

As the story goes, when Jesus was twelve years old he went with his family and his extended family up to Jerusalem for the Feast of Passover. After the feast had ended, the family group returned home. Unknown to anyone, Jesus stayed behind at the temple. At the end of the day, his parents couldn't find him amongst the cousins and friends along their journey route, so they returned to Jerusalem to look for him. Can you imagine how frantic his parents must have been?

After three days they found him in the temple courts, sitting among the teachers, listening to them and asking them questions. Everyone who heard him was amazed at his understanding and his answers.
– Luke 2: 46–47, *NIV*

In the temple, teachers came and taught in an open forum. Imagine being able to sit in on lectures from the top college professors and being able to interact with them. As Dr. David Stern explains, *"This questioning or "putting sh'eilot" was not one-sided querying but a dialogue, since Yeshua answered the rabbis' return-questions. Thus, there was a real intellectual exchange going on, and the listeners were amazed at how well this twelve-year-old was holding up his side of it."*[16]

---

[16] Page 110, Stern, David H Stern. *Jewish New Testament Commentary*, Jewish New Testament Publications, Inc., Clarksville, MD, 1992.

JESUS USED INTERACTION LIKE VERBAL SALT

The way Jesus used the interactive tools is best described with one of his analogies, "You are the salt of the earth." Interactive tools are like "verbal salt" that gives flavor, increases the appetite, preserves and makes it memorable, and kills infection or loss of the message.

Interactive techniques have four general purposes:
- Bait
- Hook
- Pushback
- Catch and Release

Each of these four principles mentioned earlier, are included in the steps for using the tools Jesus used in the interactive communication process. Here are some steps.

1. WORD PICTURES, EVERYDAY EXPERIENCES AND OBJECTS

These images help us to bait the hook, the way he did. Jesus knew his audience and used simple stories and examples that people would understand. The majority of his time was spent in the Galilean countryside, and his stories and word pictures reflected the issues that "country folk" or folks from an agrarian culture would relate to, such as:

- *A tree is recognized by its fruit.*
- *You are the light for the world.*
- *You are the salt for the Land.*
- *I am the vine and you are the branches.*
- *The eye is the lamp of the body.*
- *The Kingdom of God is like the man who found a treasure in a field.*
- *Consider the lilies of the field, how they grow; even Solomon in all his glory was not arrayed like one of these.*

Staying with the fishing analogy, consider that fish eat what they know. Fishermen know that fish can be very particular when it comes to the menu. Fish are creatures of habit, and like to eat what is familiar. So, fishermen provide bait that fit this criteria. Why? It's how to catch fish.

My friend Sandra's parents took up the hobby of fly-fishing when they retired. Sandra's dad showed me some of his lures. They were impressive. They looked so lifelike that I fully expected something would fly or jump up at us. He spent hours making these amazing miniature wingy things. Lures have to look real because the fish go after something that looks familiar and appeals to them. The same is true for people. People respond best to the familiar and appealing. They prefer to be introduced gradually to new ideas.

Some associates of mine who dabbled in the music industry discovered this principle the hard way. They were asked by a singing group to produce a new CD with all new and original songs. The singers were from a long running television variety show. One of the producers suggested that the song mix include mostly old favorites with some new material. The artists insisted on recording only their new and original songs. When the television spots for the new album premiered, the sales were underwhelming. Actually, sales were dreadful and the pallets of recordings remained in the warehouse. They discovered the reason that the Golden Oldies sell; fans want the familiar old songs from familiar artists.

LESSON OF THE FAMILIAR

Just like the parables, the interactive hooks that Jesus used incorporated familiar experiences, objects and issues. He introduced familiar topics but gave them new meaning and context, such as, "You are the light of the world." Statements like that make you think. How can that be? How am I the light of the world? What does that mean? As soon as people think about the question, they are mentally hooked and waiting for more information to consider.

2. TEACHING WITH QUESTIONS – CAST THE HOOK!

Throwing questions out is like casting the fishing line. Throughout history great teachers have used questions to teach. Questions are one of the most important tools of interaction because they can be used both to engage the audience but also to test, measure and qualify their receptivity. There are several root meanings to the word question. One of the major definitions comes from the word "quest" which means to seek out or to find. Other meanings are: scattering, a puzzle, a trick, a riddle and to "tie in a knot." This means that questions help to find answers and can also be used to puzzle or to tie things up.

Questions can be used like maps to gauge where people are mentally. Their answers help us to better understand how to connect with them. Their answers help us recognize people's needs, their concerns, their level of competency, their attitudes, their willingness to change and their corporate culture. For example, I always ask something like this, "What are the most critical issues that you would like addressed before the end of the session?" Or "What are you expectations for the session?" Another question I might ask is, "What problem would you hope to find practical solutions for in this session?"

People's responses help us determine if we need to continue, ask another question or walk away. Jesus asked questions to see if people really wanted to listen. If a person came with an open heart, he responded to them. If not, he didn't even answer.

3. OPEN-ENDED QUESTIONS HELP TO "REEL 'EM IN"

Life is made up of millions of questions. When we are asked questions, it stimulates thought and cognitive involvement. Remember when Mr. Rogers said, "Would you like to be my neighbor?" Did you say "yes" and nod your head? Mr. Roger's made us want to be his neighbor. He made us want to put on our sneakers, get comfortable and have nice friends.

WON'T YOU BE MY NEIGHBOR?

Open-ended questions make us think and respond. Salesmen do it all the time. For example, you are house hunting and the real estate agent asks, "Where would you put the piano or Christmas tree?" Very smart question, on their part. Immediately, you start mentally placing your furniture in that house. This empty house has started morphing into your home filled with happy memories.

Salesmen know that once a person starts to visualize himself or herself in the house, the car, the outfit, or wearing the ring, they are closer to closing a sale.

Jesus used open-ended questions to see how his team was doing. He asked questions like, "Who do men say I am?" "Does this offend you?" "Do you want to go away, too?" "Which is easier: to say 'Your sins are forgiven' or to say, 'Get up and walk?'"

THE ART OF THE QUESTION

Learning how to ask the right questions takes skill. Those network news anchors and reporters who ask great questions took years to develop that ability. In fact it takes an average of ten to fifteen years for a television journalist to develop the skills necessary to be a network correspondent. A big part of that training is learning how to ask questions that evoke a spontaneous response. When people feel safe, they tell us what they are really thinking and feeling. The key is learning how to ask the right questions.

QUESTIONING SUCCESS

We held a corporate training class with an I.T. group (Information Technology) that was responsible for writing software programs. In it, we presented an exercise where they had to write questions to interview a potential new offshore member to be assigned to their project. What kinds of questions did they develop? Of all the questions that the different groups came up with, over 85% were closed questions. They crafted questions that required a "yes" or "no" answer. Some of them came up with questions related to logistics.

The exercise was, "What kind of questions would you ask?" The questions they wrote gave us insight into where to start. Their work revealed where they were. So, in the class we taught people how to use questions to discover more critical aspects about a team member's strengths and work style. Within a week, the team returned with multiple success stories of improved morale and increased productivity. They mentioned how they avoided several potentially costly problems by using open-ended questions with their team members. For example, they no longer asked this kind of question: "Have you ever worked on a project like this before?" Instead they asked, "What was the last project like this that you worked on and what did you contribute to the team?"

4. PushBack – First Level of Implementation – Test the Waters!

Don't give your pearls to swine! They will trample the pearls, then turn and attack you.[17]

Going with the fishing analogy, if you see snakes swimming toward you across the water, don't throw your line in. Watch for the trap. If you see it, don't step in it. How did Jesus handle these situations? Scripture tells us not to throw our pearls before swine because they will trample them underfoot. Why? One reason could be they have no capacity to appreciate pearls. His amazingly graphic statement is probably one of the most quoted truths, especially in times of misunderstanding.

The pain of this truth resonates in many of our hearts. We all have had times when we have given our best to someone or to a project and it was not appreciated. We felt trampled. Sometimes it may be worse. What about the times you've been blamed for an outcome or were used for a verbal punching bag? Jesus teaches that we have to forgive and turn the other cheek. But he did not teach that we have to absorb the verbal abuse, anger and frustration of other people – especially when someone is looking for a fight.

A friend of mine, Gwen, told me about several conversations where she was set up. The person would ask her a question about an issue and then use the conversation to vent their frustrations to Gwen. The person came "asking" for help, but in truth they just wanted to use someone as a place to vent, dump, gossip or hammer opinions. Encounters like this are draining and deplete our emotional resources and time. To help Gwen protect herself, we created some questions that she could use to test a person's motives and establish some guidelines.

---

[17] Page. 54, *The Life of Jesus*, Tyndale House Publishing, Inc., Wheaton, IL, 2004.

For example, if someone came and asked, "What do you think about this issue or something that happened?" Before answering, test the waters with a question like, "What is your response?" "How are you feeling about it?" "What is your take on it?" "Why do you want to know?"

If you can tell from their answers that the person wants to complain or gossip, then it is best to avoid or divert the conversation.

We hear the term "boundaries." We hear that we need to establish them. But how can we do it and, at the same time, turn the other cheek? The way Jesus did this was to ask questions before responding. He tested what was on their minds and in their hearts before engaging.

Once someone in the crowd shouted to Jesus, "Teacher, tell my brother to divide the inheritance with me."

Jesus said, "Who made me the judge over you?" Rather than getting caught in a dispute that was not his to decide, Jesus deflected the question and answered with a parable about a rich young ruler who discovers that his life is shorter than he expected. – Luke 12: 13–21

With his question and parable, Jesus reflected the issue of the inheritance and established God as the judge over all earthly blessings. Jesus didn't waste his time arguing with people. He asked questions to avoid no-win situations as well as to test the motives and agenda of others.

APPLICATION

Often, people ask a question but they really don't want an answer. They may be looking for a shoulder to cry on, or for someone to listen. They may be looking for someone who supports their opinion. They may want to take out their anger on some unsuspecting person. This is why you need to be aware and ask open-ended questions. Listen to the responses. The information will help you determine whether or not to proceed. Don't be a dump, vent, or punching bag.

There are many different scenarios and script possibilities that you can follow, but for the workplace, here are a few of the common ones. If the person is a friend, then make sure that it is a good time to talk. Try to bring them around to being solution-minded and being empowered to change their situation.

If the person is a known complainer, direct him/her to a supervisor or someone who can help find a solution. Ask him/her what a possible solution would be. If he/she doesn't have one, say you would be happy to talk once you've had more time to think about it. If the person has a legitimate problem, direct him/her to someone who can assist with his or her work, personal or spiritual problems. Just as it is pointless to go fishing in a mud puddle, neither can you expect to have a meaningful exchange with someone who is shallow and wants to play tennis with cow patties.

5. Using Questions to Prequalify and Test the Weight

Many game fishermen practice catch-and-release. After catching the fish, they weigh and measure it before releasing it back into the lake or stream. Other game fishermen keep the fish if they are over a certain weight and size. When we ask questions, it helps us determine the weight or level of a person's need. The person's answer may reveal he is not interested in learning anything from us, but a sincere, genuine answer is compelling and stirs a response. A question can help us measure the response and decide whether to continue with a conversation.

When individuals want something from us, we don't need to feel obliged to give it to them. As the previous examples demonstrated, asking questions is a great pushback technique that helps evaluate the intent as well as the need of the person making the requests. Once we evaluate the intent we can weigh the need and respond accordingly. Questions are a great measuring tool to protect us from time-wasters.

In business there are hundreds of time-wasters. One of the biggest complaints of corporate employees is spending time in unnecessary meetings. Even though you may not always have a choice about attending certain meetings, using questions to prequalify the request is a helpful tool.

At the beginning of my career, I asked a successful entrepreneur, who I had assisted in the past, for a meeting about a project. Before he made a commitment, he asked a series of questions. He wanted to know the reason for the meeting, the objectives, what stage my project was in, how I thought he could help, and what might be the benefit and time frame. Frankly, I was shocked and slightly offended. I felt nervous. In my naïve presumption, I never considered that he wouldn't schedule the meeting, especially since I had a positive history with him. What I quickly realized was how focused he and his professional team were about his time. If my request for a meeting didn't meet his standard of productivity, no matter how much he liked me, he didn't have time to meet. I got the meeting and it went well. Today, what I appreciated most was how he used a model of questions to protect his schedule from time-wasters.

TIME FOR A "TIME-WASTER"

Jesus dealt with many crowds. He determined with whom to interact. Sometimes people were considered time-wasters by others, but not by Jesus. A blind beggar in Jericho heard Jesus was passing by. He cried out, "Jesus, Son of David, have mercy on me!"

The man showed boldness calling Jesus by one of the names of the promised Messiah. Crying out "Son of David" could have caused him serious trouble. If a Roman solider heard, someone might get killed. The people around him said, "Shut up if you know what's good for ya'." He refused, and kept calling out. He was so loud and insistent that Jesus had them bring him through the crowd.

Jesus asked him one basic question, "What do you want Me to do for you?"

"Lord," he said, "I want to see!"

"Receive your sight!" Jesus told him. "Your faith has healed you."
– Luke 18: 35–43, *HCBC*.

In this exchange, Jesus asked the blind man a question that tested his intent and intensity. The blind man's passion overcame the verbal obstacle to declare his faith and proclaim his hope. He gave a simple answer in a voice that was probably quivering with emotion. Jesus responded immediately and Jesus gave him his heart's desire.

DID JESUS USE VISUAL PROPS?

Visual aids and props are dynamite teaching tools, which is why I believe that Jesus often used them. Familiar objects could easily have been within reach when he spoke. When Jesus saw a widow putting all she had, two mites, into the offering box at the temple, he commented on what a huge gift she gave. It is easy to imagine the disciples looking around at each other wondering if they had missed something. This old woman left only a tiny offering. Jesus went on to say that the widow, who was poor, gave all she had to live on, while others had given only a bit out of their wealth.

Jesus used a simple act with simple, available verbal props to establish a critical, spiritual principle and to affirm positive behavior. When positive behavior is affirmed, it reproduces itself. In any environment, Kudos and "Shout Outs" only take a few minutes but they leave huge long-term impressions toward building morale and improving performance. Jesus gave a simple, genuine compliment that affirmed the compassion behind the action.

Props are a great teaching tool for many reasons. First of all they use a whole brain approach to communication. Working with objects uses different parts of our brain. Seeing an object, we remember physical sensations. We may recall how to use it. We might think of how it feels to touch it. It stimulates muscles, emotions, logic and memories. Using familiar objects makes the story and the message even more memorable. In the future, whenever people encounter the same experience or object, they will be reminded of the story and the information. The use of interactive and whole brain learning techniques is the same reason that Montessori classrooms or home schooling is so successful with some students.

APPLICATION

Props help to attract and retain audience attention. Props increase audience participation because they use whole brain communication to learn.

The Joy of Riddles

In the movie and the book, *I Robot*, the story begins with the murder of a prominent scientist who has left a hologram message for the detective assigned to his case. The detective, played by Will Smith, unsuccessfully questions the hologram about the homicide. Finally the hologram replies, "That is the *right question!*" Even though the hologram cannot identify the murderer, the correct question points the detective in the right direction, so the planet is saved.

Riddles are simple mysteries waiting to be unlocked. Games and stories are based on questions that stretch and tease our brain. I love the show *Car Talk*, especially when they have the "Brain Puzzler" section. Check out this PBS radio show on the weekends. The Auto Mechanic brothers answer phone-in questions about any vehicle, running or not. Who would have thought that car questions would be fun and entertaining?

Jesus used riddles that communicated spiritual principles through simple objects. Rather than give lengthy theological or philosophical arguments, he used a riddle to explain.

> Blessed are the poor in spirit, for the Kingdom of Heaven is theirs,
>
> How blessed are those who mourn! For they will be comforted.
>
> Blessed are the pure in heart for they will see God.

Even if you did not understand the riddles Jesus taught, they made an impression. Even today people are still trying to unlock the mysteries they contain. For practical application, riddles are great to use in appropriate situations. They work beautifully for media interviews, as long as you can give the answer in a concise manner. Riddles are terrific icebreakers for a meeting or training session.

Showdown in the Temple Corral!

One of the best examples of Jesus using questions was in the final public showdown at the Temple Complex during the last week of his life. Jesus had arrived in Jerusalem for Passover festivals and taught in the temple courtyards. All of a sudden the big guys showed up, chief priests, scribes, and elders, and challenged him about teaching.

Jesus was popular because his teaching made sense. He gave simple revelation. His explanations of the spiritual laws made them easier to understand and live by. Instead of layers and layers of rituals, he gave people a simple explanation and a path to build a relationship with the Father. In our terms, it would be like having a flat rate income tax. (Oh, let me take a few moments to dream about that possibility. Imagine simpler forms, corporations really paying taxes with silly loopholes gone, more rest, less audits and trees saved.)

There were rules. One was that unless you belonged to the clubhouse, as a rabbi you weren't allowed to present any new interpretations of the law while teaching in the temple complex. (I'm sure that they had to get lesson plans approved by the committees also.) But Jesus had been shaking things up since he arrived in town the day before. It had started with the donkey ride – the crowd doing the "wave" with the palm fronds and greenery. The people had cheered him.

Then Jesus nearly started a riot when he whupped the moneychangers, who'd scattered out of the temple like angry roosters. Imagine shutting down the merchants during the busiest season of the year. Consider how much revenue that was normally made during the High Holiday. The Chief Priests were not happy campers. After that business settled down, the children ran around singing, "Hosanna to the Son of David." It must have seemed like total mayhem.

Jesus left to spend the night with his friend Lazarus whom they say he raised from the dead. Now, it was day two. Jesus was back teaching in the complex.

The chief priests, scribes and elders came to confront Jesus because he crossed several lines. *"By what authority are you doing these things? Who gave you this authority?"* The leaders wanted to know what kind of ordination Jesus had received that entitled him to teach and present new points of the law, as well as disturb the peace of the temple.[18] (Ok, Jesus,

---

[18] Page 64 *Jewish New Testament Commentary.*

show us the diplomas. Where's your license? And whom do you work for really?)

Jesus responded, "I will ask you one question. If you answer it for Me, then I will tell you by what authority I do these things. Where did John's authority come from? From heaven or from men?"

Brilliant question and it threw the leaders into chaos. They began to argue among themselves, "If we say, 'From heaven,' He will say to us, 'Then why didn't you believe him?' But if we say, 'From men,' we're afraid of the crowd, because everyone believes John was a prophet." So they answered Jesus, "We don't know."

And He said to them, "Neither will I tell you by what authority I do these things." – Matthew 21: 23–26, *HCBC*

What an amazing exchange. It was a throw down and the new comer from a backwater hick town came out on top. Who could have imagined? Jesus shut down the most brilliant minds in the nation with a single question. It was checkmate, game over and out.

When the leaders refused to respond to his question, Jesus continued to teach. What he had done was reframe the argument so that his opponents could not respond. Instead of defending his actions, he turned the truth mirror around, and his opponents ran from their own reflection. It was like turning the light on in the kitchen at night and watching the bugs scatter.

Even though Jesus won the confrontation, this was the catalyst that pushed things over the edge. When he made the moneychangers waltz with the whip, it shook things up one too many times. You can talk all you want but when you start messing with people's pocketbooks, you better get ready for a fight. In life, you don't want to fight city hall, the Supreme Court or the IRS. Unfortunately Jesus crossed the line with the equivalent of all three. The different leaders of the religious establishment hated him. They began working together to eliminate him. But when it came to questions and confrontation, Jesus was unbeatable.

APPLICATION

Disconnection and avoidance are the best policy when you find yourself in an ugly confrontation. Remember, you don't have an obligation to answer questions from people who want to fight. Instead use their own arguments to pin them down. Know their weakness and point it out. If you can get the dog to chase its tail...it will not have time to bite you.

ARE YOU REALLY LISTENING? "IF YOU HAVE EARS THEN LISTEN UP!"

Communication is difficult. Even though we choose great stories, use terrific jokes, write concise sound bites, conduct research and carefully craft a memo that addresses the heartfelt needs of our audience, it may be all in vain. Things happen. Sometimes the seed grows. Sometimes it doesn't. We can't make people listen. They have a choice. But we can try to communicate in a manner that is interesting and compelling.

When Jesus used parables he did not feel obligated to explain them. He did, however, give a disclaimer and reminded his audience, time and time again, "He who has ears to hear, let him listen." He often told people to listen carefully, and asked them if they were really listening to what he was saying. Jesus made people responsible for what they heard. If they didn't want to listen, he released them.

In the southwest you would probably hear Jesus saying – if you have ears, then listen up!

Who knows where the "listen up" phrase first came from? It's dreadful grammar, but such a colorful phrase. In the Land of the Rodeo, if you hear the term "listen up," you are probably in church or at a football game. Listen up, reminds me of cowboy movies, John Wayne and wagon trains. Listen up reminds me of saddle up, which means jump on your horse and be ready to ride. Listen up reminds me of reach up, which is what a child does with her daddy. Listen up reminds me of the words St. John heard from heaven, "come up here."

So what does listen up mean? Listen up means to pull the wax out of your ears and lift yourself up to the next level of understanding. Jesus didn't give answers to his riddles or endings to his stories. Instead he left people with more questions, which would

Now, there was about this time Jesus, a wise man, if it be lawful to call him a man, for he was a doer of wonderful works – a teacher of such men as receive the truth with pleasure. He drew over to him both many of the Jews, and many of the Gentiles. He was (the) Christ; and when Pilate, at the suggestion of the principal men amongst us, had condemned him to the cross, those that loved him at the first did not forsake him, for he appeared to them alive again the third day, as the divine prophets had foretold these and ten thousand other wonderful things concerning him; and the tribe of Christians, so named from him, are not extinct at this day.

Josephus, The Antiquities of the Jews, Book 18, Ch.3.3

make them search for the answers. Perhaps this is what he meant by being salt and light? If we are to be salty in our communication, does that mean that people will seek answers? And if we are to be light, then will it help people think more clearly?

RETIRING STORY

My friends, Bob and Barbara conducted a Christian musical program at a retirement community with Alzheimer's patients. After they finished, they asked the supervisor how she thought it went since the group had seemed rather subdued. The supervisor was thrilled, "It was the best one we've had. No one fell asleep." What a way to measure success!

SUMMARY

Master Communicators use interaction to give their presentations impact. Like the doors on a house, interaction helps people enter into the message. Interaction can also be used to pushback and defend. The way Jesus used interactive tools is best described with one of his analogies, "You are the salt of the earth." Interaction is like "verbal salt" that gives flavor, increases the appetite, preserves (and makes it memorable), and kills infection or loss of the message. Interaction can also bring out the best in us, like Mr. Rogers, "Will you be my neighbor?"

Interactive tools help to make things stick in people's minds and activate their understanding. In a world with too little time, it is important not to waste energy on sending messages that aren't being received or people who aren't interested. Jesus gave the world the phrase, "Don't throw your pearls before swine." It is the fruitful vine, the faithful servant that is celebrated.

Jesus was concerned with planting his seeds of truth in good soil. He taught important information in private meetings with his followers. He didn't waste the "good stuff" on the negative crowds and those of hard head and heart. The lesson to remember is that when it came to critical and precious information, Jesus didn't throw his seed on the concrete and neither should we.

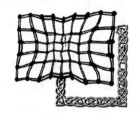

CHAPTER 6
MULTI-TRACK – EXPANDING THE NET
(TO MAKE A LASTING IMPRESSION)

The most powerful communicators in the world know how to weave their message and stories into a net that captures audiences' attention. The third technique of the S.I.M.P.L.E.™ Method is the use of multi-track communication. All people communicate on different levels simultaneously. Like the different instruments in an orchestra, the multiple tracks of communication work together to transmit information. There are five diverse tracks, which are the physical, emotional, intellectual, intuitive and spiritual levels. Jesus used multi-track communication to expand his communication impact and make it more memorable.

The understanding that we have of the world is our religion. Everyone has a religion, whether he formally belongs to a church or not.
– M. Scott Peck, M.D.

Think of one of your favorite movies or TV shows. What makes you want to watch it again and again? Is it the story, the action, the actors, the directing, the cinematography, the music, or the special effects? How do you feel after you watch it? What do you remember most? Do certain scenes play over and over again in your head?

A great movie is wonderful because all the layers of images, sound, stories, and people are carefully woven together. A great movie depends on the editor to give it life. The editor is the final maestro who takes the thousand upon thousand of images, sounds, and visual effects and places them in sequence. An editor must be a builder, timekeeper, artist and juggler. First and foremost, the editor's job is to tell the story by arranging the images so that they make sense to the audience. Editors once used razors and converted laundry bins to assemble a film. Now computers and mega memory processors help them assemble and build.

Electronic communication, whatever it may be, a movie, a commercial, a web page, a PowerPoint presentation or a music recording, is composed of multiple layers of information. Even though the layering and compressing of thousands of images by the media is revolutionary, the concept is ancient. From the Greeks to Shakespeare to Broadway, thespians in every culture understand the importance of multi-track communication.

EXPAND THE NET

Multi-track application is the third technique of the S.I.M.P.L.E.™ Method. Multi-track communication broadens and deepens the quality of a message. Like expanding the size of a billboard, multi-track communication makes information memorable by reinforcing the message or enlarging it. Stories are like fishing lines or baskets that unite the raw content of a message. Interaction helps to attract, stimulate and hook the audience into listening. Multi-track communication helps to keep people involved because the layers and complexity make a story more interesting.

For example, you many not care about watching a program about lawyers, but if the story is about something of interest you may sit down and watch. In the S.I.M.P.L.E.™ Method, the story is a single net. Interactions are hooks and bait. The Multi-Track technique is like a larger drag net because it expands, widens and deepens the opportunity for a catch. Using a building analogy, stories are like the rooms in a house. Interaction is the way you get into the house. It's the doors and the sidewalk. Multi-track gives people a reason to visit and makes them want to stay.

THE COMPLEXITY OF COMMUNICATION

Communication is more than noise or simple sound. It is complex because like a psychic orchestra, it comes from all parts of us – the body, the soul and the spirit. We tend to think of communication as a matter of the mind and will, but **communication is an intrinsic convergence of everything we are**. It is made up of what we do, what we say, what we sing, how we feel, what we desire, what we hope and what we dream.

Movies and television have made us all excellent judges of the subtext of people's conversations. We watch to see if the guilty murderer will twitch at the detective's question. We measure the sincerity of a lover's pledge. While it is easy to read the many layers of messages in someone else's conversation, it is not as easy to recognize and control our own.

In the corporate world we take tests to help us understand the personalities, work styles, communication styles, strengths and shortcomings of the members of our teams. The successes of our team efforts depend on how well we utilize the strengths, talents and abilities of our group. Some of the people who make up the group may be very logical, task oriented, left brain thinkers; others may be more relational, creative, right brain thinkers. Neither is better than the other, but when the strengths of the individuals work in harmony, then it brings out the best of everyone.

THE FIVE LEVELS OF MULTI-TRACK COMMUNICATION

ALL PEOPLE ARE MULTI-TRACK COMMUNICATORS

Along with different types of thinking styles and personalities, people have different communication styles from introverted to extroverted. Some are direct. Others are passive and sensitive. Some are expressive while others are detailed oriented or skeptical. In our training, we use well-known corporate tests that identify a person's communication style. Becoming aware of one's communication style helps people learn how to maximize their strengths and minimize their weaknesses, while adapting to the needs, language and style of their co-workers, clients and bosses.

No matter the communication style, all people are multi-track communicators. There are five communication tracks that we all use to send, receive, filter and decipher messages.

The five multi-track levels are:

Physical, Emotional, Intellectual, Intuitive and Spiritual.

PHYSICAL track includes the five senses of taste, smell, sight, sound and touch. The physical also includes our gender, and our biological and genetic makeup.

EMOTIONAL track involves all matters relating to the heart, feelings, emotions, memories and relationships.

INTELLECTUAL track relates to the mind, which includes the intellect, logic, reason, facts, observations and knowledge.

INTUITIVE describes the "gut feelings" or instincts that relate to basic needs, flight or fight response and survival.

SPIRITUAL track involves personal values, beliefs, truth, spiritual understanding and inspiration that direct a person's life.

MULTI-TRACK COMMUNICATION

Physical – Five Senses, Gender, Genes

Heart – Emotions, Memories, Relationships

Head – Intellect, Reason, Logic, Facts, Observation

Gut – Experience, Needs, Opinions, Survival

Spirit – Truth, Morals, Values, Inspiration

The levels should seem familiar since they come from basic psychology. Even though we are aware of something, it doesn't mean that we know how to use it. Just like remembering to turn on the front porch light or to use the "clean disk tool," the familiar can be unintentionally forgotten.

The five communication tracks work together like the five fingers on a hand to help us hold onto thoughts and information. These are woven together like fabric and impact each other. Each person integrates and uses these tracks, consciously or unconsciously, every time they communicate. The goal is to learn to use each of these tracks effectively.

Just as we all have different thumbprints or voiceprints, we all have unique communication styles. Even though we all are born with the same communication toolbox, we don't all use the tools with the same level of skill. Our personalities, culture, genetics, education, training, jobs, experience, age and dozens of other factors contribute to how we use them.

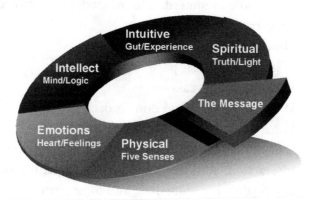

LEVEL FIVE COMMUNICATORS

It is easy to recognize a great communicator. Like holding all the reins for a team of horses, the Master Communicator works with all five-communication tracks. It takes energy and skill to get everything pointed in the right direction. Examples have to support the facts and the images have to support the emotions.

Talk show hosts, TV journalists, movie stars, politicians, recording artists, CEOs, professional speakers, and spokespersons work on developing and refining the use of the five communication tracts. They analyze, practice, write, rewrite, edit, rehearse and rehearse some more. When you have only twenty seconds on camera, you want to make it your best. Whether it is a sound bite supporting orphans in Africa, an iPod interview or a walk down the red carpet, there is pressure to be as precise and as perfect as possible. One wrong comment or remark can end a career or be a five star blooper on the Internet.

LET'S EVALUATE

So how do we integrate and use more multi-track communication techniques? The first way to start is to evaluate one of your presentations. Take a few seconds and review a presentation, a speech, an interview, a lesson or a sermon that you gave. Briefly, answer the following questions:

- What was the purpose of the presentation?
- Was it work required, sales related, inspirational, or instructional?
- How happy were you with the results?
- What was the best part?
- What was the weakest?
- What do I wish I had done more of?
- What do I wish I had done less of?
- Rate your use of examples, stories, facts, humor, interaction, audience participation, organization, and feedback – immediate and long term.
- How did the audience benefit and what did they take away?
- Which of the five multi-track levels are you most comfortable with?
- Which ones do you need to work on?

Audience feedback and comments can also be an important source of evaluating yourself.

JESUS – COMMUNICATION COACH

There are many ways to learn multi-track communication, but one of the best is to see it modeled. Jesus used multi-track communication continually. That is one reason why his teachings have such life. The parables, teachings, similes and questions all have multiple layers of meaning and tracks to explore.

The Prodigal (Lost) Son

Jesus connected on all levels by masterful use of stories. Learning to connect on all the levels takes work and skill. The story of the Prodigal Son is one of the most familiar and retold stories from the Bible. Like all great stories it is successful because it connects on all five of the multi-track levels. Here is the version found in *THE MESSAGE Bible*:

There was once a man who had two sons. The younger said to his father, "Father, I want right now what's coming to me."

So the father divided the property between them. It wasn't long before the younger son packed his bags and left for a distant country. There, undisciplined and dissipated, he wasted everything he had. After he had gone through all his money, there was a bad famine all through that country and he began to hurt. He signed on with a citizen there who assigned him to his fields to slop the pigs. He was so hungry he would have eaten the corncobs in the pig slop. But no one would give him any.

"That brought him to his senses. He said, "All those farmhands working for my father sit down to three meals a day, and here I am starving to death. I'm going back to my father, I'll say to him, 'Father, I've sinned against God, I've sinned before you; I don't deserve to be called your son. Take me on as a hired hand.' He got right up and went home to his father.

"When he was still a long way off, his father saw him. His heart pounding, he ran out, embraced him, and kissed him. The son started his speech; "Father, I've sinned against God, I've sinned before you; I don't deserve to be called your son ever again."

"But the father wasn't listening. He was calling to the servants. "Quick. Bring a clean set of clothes and dress him. Put the family ring on his finger and sandals on his feet. Then get a grain-fed heifer and roast it. We're going to feast! We're going to have a wonderful time! My son is here – given up for dead and now alive! Given up for lost and now found!" And they began to have a wonderful time.

"All this time his older son was out in the field. When the day's work was done he came in. As he approached the house, he heard the music and dancing. Calling over one of the houseboys, he asked what was going on. He told him, "Your brother came home. Your father has ordered a feast – barbecued beef! – because he has him home safe and sound."

"The older brother stalked off in an angry sulk and refused to join in. His father came out and tried to talk to him, but he wouldn't listen. The son said, "Look how many years I've stayed here serving you, never giving you one moment of grief, but have you ever thrown a party for me and my friends? Then this son of yours who has thrown away your money on whores shows up and you go all out with a feast!

"His father said, 'Son you don't understand. You're with me all the time, and everything that is mine is yours – but this is a wonderful time, and we had to celebrate. This brother of yours was dead, and he's alive! He was lost, and he's found!' "[19]

– Luke 15: 11–31,[20] *THE MESSAGE*

Jesus used stories that captured the hearts and the universal emotions of people. The story of the prodigal son has been retold in hundreds of different ways. We relate to the story because most of us have walked through a prodigal season, or have a child or relative who are prodigals. Parents understand the heartbreak of a child wasting his life and inheritance in foolish activities. And even if the prodigal has not returned home, there is still hope that someday he will return.

In telling this story, Jesus did more than share a soap opera plot, he was communicating deep spiritual truths. The intent of the story was to help each person realize that the Father in Heaven is waiting and hoping and longing and looking every minute to see if the dust from the distant road is giving the signal that his children are coming home to where they belong.

[19] *THE MESSAGE*, The New Testament, Eugene H. Peterson, NavPress Publishing Group, Colorado Springs, CO, 1993.
[20] *THE MESSAGE*.

MULTI-TRACK STORYTELLING

Great storytellers know the beauty of a great story and how to tell it. Let's return to the saga of the Prodigal and see how Jesus modeled multi-track communication to touch people simultaneously on all five levels.

PHYSICAL – This story is full of sensory images. From feasting with the prostitutes to slopping the pigs, to the joyous hug of this father, this story connects to all five of the senses. We can imagine the lifestyle, shudder at the work. (Whew, try not to breathe deeply because of the smell.) We can almost hear his stomach growling louder than the pigs'. We can imagine the long walk home from the foreign land and the sound of his father running to greet him. Can you hear the father's cries, choked with emotion? Can you feel the joyous hug? And there is nothing like the smell of good barbeque and a fatted prime calf roast.

HEART – This story is filled with a wide range of emotions. It is easy to feel the emotions of the son and how he changes from the arrogant son to the repentant servant. Imagine the thrill of the father's disappointment and sorrow turning to joy at his son's return. All of us can relate to having a conflict with a brother and not being understood. Some may find the father's remarkable outpouring of love at the repentance of his son disturbing. Some may relate to the resentment of the older brother.

HEAD – The facts relating to this story are not detailed but are enough so that we can understand the motivations, attitudes, conflicts and issues. The scenario is familiar enough that we can fill in the details with the faces, finances and situations. By not telling us the outcome with the offended older brother, it makes us ask, "Then what happened?"

INTUITIVE – We all have experienced family conflict, failure, and the need for repentance. In our gut, we understand the truth of this story because most of us have played all the roles at one time or another. We know intuitively how difficult it was for the prodigal to

The story of the Prodigal son is a classic but what is a prodigal? We know one when we see one, but what does the word really mean? Prodigal comes from the Latin meaning to drive forth, to lavish. It also means profuse, liberal, and excessive. It has come to represent a person who spends his life and his money extravagantly or one who leaves his home. In our culture, a prodigal also describes runaways, the rebellious and someone who has lost his way. It is also associated with a drug user, an alcoholic, or a sex addict. This story may be about a son who was lost, but the story is also "prodigal" for it is lavish and profuse with meaning and symbolism.

face his failures, how much the father's heart grieved and how perplexed the older brother must have been.

SPIRITUAL – This story has a basic plot line but it was meant to communicate much deeper truths and principles. Some of those are: the vanity of false values, the folly of pride, the love of the Father, the power of envy, and how we can become disconnected from what is most important.

USE MENTAL VELCRO – MULTI-TRACK APPLICATION

When we use a multi-track approach it helps to give our messages lasting impact. The quality and craft with which the message is shaped will impact the response of the audience. In order to communicate effectively, whether on the news, in the office or at home, it is important that we learn to adapt to the new communication rules of our society. We don't often have time to tell a whole story. Sometimes we may only have thirty seconds with our boss, or a seven-second sound bite or a five-word email header. The key is learning to use multi-track communication even when you have a time or word limit.

One of the phrases that we use to explain these strategies is called "Weaving Mental Velcro™." Invented for space travel, Velcro is one of the most useful products of our time. Anyone who has to deal with a toddler's shoes, a display unit, some sports equipment or a thousand other loose gadgets can be grateful for this invention. In the universe of information, with maxed out mental RAM, it is critical to help thoughts stick in people's minds. When we weave memorable images, stories, analogies, phrases into our presentations, it helps ensure that the messages and information we are imparting will stick in someone's memory.

Examples of "Mental Velcro" can be both short and long. Advertisers spend millions researching and creating slogans, jingles and images that will make you buy their brand. Think, McDonalds, Pepsi, Ford Trucks and Geico. Politicians use Mental Velcro for mailers and speeches. Think – "I feel your pain!" or "A thousand points of light." Journalists use Mental Velcro in assembling a news-cast and headlines. Television programmers build the story lines of every comedy, drama or reality based show with Mental Velcro. Filmmakers weave layers of information into a vast matrix that they hope will extract money from our pockets. These moments of "Mental Velcro" influence our society and like vast ocean currents change the paradigms of entire continents.

Jesus threw out more sound bites and "Mental Velcro" than we can imagine. Some of these are like hooks and interactive techniques, mentioned in the previous chapter. They are also powerful principles that have stood the test of time. Maybe we should call them Velcro Principles. Some examples are:

- A tree is known by its fruit.
- Can a blind guide the blind, or won't both fall in the pit?
- Don't judge and you won't be judged.
- Ask and it will be given, seek and you will find, knock and the door will be opened.
- Forgive and you will be forgiven.
- Blessed are the peacemakers for they will be called Sons of God.

APPLICATION

Use more Mental Velcro when communicating. Remember it takes time to prepare and develop these phrases, principles, stories or images, but it is worth it. Before media appearances and business presentations, take time to identify and practice these sound bites, phrases and explanations. Try them out ahead of time to see which ones people respond to and remember. You will be able to tell because their eyes will light up when a good one is mentioned. Time preparing pays off.

Don't always spoon feed your audience or give them all the answers. Students and employees, especially at the beginning of a presentation can be inspired to do their own work. Making people think about the questions will be like giving them Mental Velcro that sticks in their minds, hearts and spirits. When they have to arrive at conclusions and work for the answers, they won't soon forget them. And they'll come back for more.

A powerful agent is the right word. Whenever we come upon one of those intensely right words in a book or a newspaper the resulting effect is physical as well as spiritual, and electrically prompt. – Mark Twain

LET'S GET PHYSICAL! – THE POWER OF SENSES

Where the spirit does not work with the hand, there is no art.
– Leonardo Da Vinci

In our busy world it is easy to forget that seeing a dozen roses in the popup ad is nothing like the beauty, touch, scent and feelings that come from having fresh flowers on the table. Think about it! What have you missed about your life lately? (If you need to put this book down and take a walk outside then by all means, do it.)

Genius comes not from great deeds but grows from the power of observation. The greatest minds of history – Einstein, Shakespeare, Newton and Van Gogh – all were curious students of life. Leonardo Da Vinci wrote that one of his chief contributions and functions in life was to be an observer. Children demonstrate an insatiable appetite for learning with their senses, which adults need to imitate.

Our physical body is a gift with amazing capabilities. Unfortunately, the demands of the techno-electro-media-connecto world keeps many of us from listening to our bodies. We live, drive, eat, talk, work, and think so fast that we miss the best life has to offer. We have to switch gears out of the virtual tomorrow and start experiencing the present. Communicators help people live in real time. They give the audience a touchstone so the audience can reconnect to the world around them. When we are aware of our senses, really aware, we live more fully.

Jesus used images that stimulated the senses and helped to reconnect people to the joy of life. He talked about the wildflowers, the wind, the harvest, the sheep and about eating. The Sermon on the Mount contains some of the most simple and vivid sensory images ever used.

Which of you, if his son asks for bread, will give him a stone? Or if he asks for a fish, will give him a snake: If you, then, though you are evil, know how to give good gifts to your children, how much more will your Father in heaven give good gifts to those who ask him!
– Matthew 7: 10, *NIV*

APPLICATION

In the Prodigal Son story, images are stark and honest. We can see, feel, taste, touch and hear them. To integrate more senses into a presentation about this story you could also try using questions like the following: What would a great party be like? What sort of parties did the prodigal son go to? Who was on the guest list? Have you ever worked on a farm? What about slopping pigs? Imagine working with animals that will bite and stampede you if you get in the way of their food. Imagine the smell of an open sewer that you have to walk through and you get to sleep right beside it. How would that smell and feel?

LIVING FROM THE HEART

To wear your heart on your sleeve isn't a very good plan; you should wear it inside, where it functions best.
– Margaret Thatcher

Many of us would like to live from our hearts but we have forgotten where we put them. Disappointment, pain, rejection, misunderstanding, failure, guilt and a thousand other reasons cause many to bury their true heart behind veils of false confidence or denial. We have all disconnected from our feelings many times and for many reasons. Lies act like gatekeepers that keep our thoughts ensnared in destructive cycles. Regardless of why we are trapped or what has imprisoned us, true courage comes when we are willing to feel the pain and release the ghosts of the past from the graves of our bad memories.

Often, we find courage as we live through the emotional challenges and victories of others. Walking through their struggles and joys help us to recognize our own ghosts. It helps us learn to release them.

Master Communicators take people on a path that offers emotional release and empowerment. Jesus knew this and used stories that anyone could grasp. The Prodigal Son story has many layers of emotion to consider. It all depends which chair you choose to sit in.

Looking through the eyes of the prodigal we see the pride, the arrogance, the waste and the depravity. We see destitution that leads to desperation, and finally repentance, and returning for restoration.

Looking through the eyes of the older brother we see steadiness, commitment, the amazement, the shock, the offense, the bitterness, the anger, and the grumbling and recognition.

Looking through the eyes of the Father we see the love, the hope, the release, the sadness, the sorrow, the depression, the longing, the waiting, the recognition, the joy, the forgiveness, the restoration and the celebration.

APPLICATION

Great stories with real emotions teach us to live by example. Great stories push people to new levels when people allow themselves to be pulled into the conflict. To help involve the audience this is a great time to use open-ended questions that have people imagining the feelings, motivations and thoughts of the people in the story. For example: What would motivate a younger son to ask for his inheritance and leave? Have you ever totally blown it and didn't want anyone to know it? What must he have felt like before coming home?

GETTING AHEAD OF THINGS

We have truth at a cheap rate now; but how soon the market may rise we do not know. Truth is not always available at the same price. We must buy it at any cost but sell it on no terms.

– William Gurnall[21]

The Information Age has put all of our lives on hyper-drive. Even the rhythm and timing of the ways that we receive and assimilate information has changed. We are used to short bursts of information, complete with graphics and pictures. Even television commercials split the thirty seconds into half so they can run double the amount of advertising in the same amount of time.

This has also changed the way we talk and learn. For presenting to today's audiences, several important approaches maximize audience response. Think and prepare with concentrated bursts of information:

- Think Headlines – Start with your best information first.
- Get to the Point – Just the facts, Miss, so I don't get bored.
- Give Instant Education – Give summaries that fill in all the blanks.

[21] William Gurnall, *The Christian in Complete Armour, Daily Reading in Spiritual Warfare*, James S. Bell, Moody Press, Chicago, IL, June 2, 1994.

- Repetition Counts – It is ok to repeat yourself as long as you say it differently.
- Front load Information – Use the best stuff first in media interviews.

Jesus followed the same pattern with his storytelling techniques. At times it was like he was speaking in headlines followed by multiple metaphors and analogies to make key points.

During the well-known teaching, Sermon on the Mount, Jesus used repetition and a type of headline to drive points home. For instance, he introduced a series of principles with the same opening words, "Blessed are the" (poor in spirit, meek, peacemakers, pure in heart, etc.). This technique, which is often used in speeches, makes the points easier for the audience to follow and remember. See, The Beatitudes, Matt. 5: 3–10.

To make sure that people paid attention to a key point, Jesus would use the ending phrase, "He who has ears to hear" which gave the crowd a verbal cue. Sometimes, Jesus would repeat phrases three times, such as "He who has ears, let him hear."

Another instance, when asked about John the Baptist, Jesus asked the same questions three times, *"What did you go out in the wilderness to see?"* – Luke 7: 24–27.

In another teaching about faith Jesus used multiple images in succession. To paraphrase a passage in Luke 12: *Don't worry about your life, consider the birds, consider the wildflowers, they don't strive so stop fretting because the Father cares.*

APPLICATION

Facts and information give structure to a message. It is important that they be organized and presented in a logical and interesting manner. Like bullet points in a PowerPoint presentation, repetition helps the audience retain information. By using different metaphors and analogies about the same topic, it increases the impact and helps reinforce the principles in the listeners' minds.

GIVING "INSTANT EDUCATION"

In dealing with the 21st century audience who are addicted

to information and wisdom, it is important to provide them with "Instant Education." This means that speakers, teachers, trainers, and interviewees need to provide their audience with interesting and relevant information and facts along with quick summaries of books, issues or current events. During his life, Dr. Edwin Louis Cole was considered one of the best teachers in ministry circles. Early in his career he had television experience that trained him to teach a principle a minute in his presentations. He presented take-away information at the beginning instead of the end.

APPLICATION

Work to streamline and concentrate your message by using bullet points, instant education and getting to the point and principles more quickly. Forget back loading or getting to the most important information later. Front load your essential information, especially for media interviews. Remember that the electronic media has compressed and layered information into new packages. Because of this, people expect public communicators to be more proficient. People expect more stories, facts and "news they can use."

GO WITH YOUR GUT!

When I examine myself and my methods of thought, I come to the conclusion that the gift of fantasy has meant more to me than my talent for absorbing positive knowledge.
– Albert Einstein

Have you ever had a gut feeling? Ever have butterflies in the stomach before giving a speech? Did you ever make a decision about someone before you looked at the resume? Have you ever followed a hunch? Did you ever take a turn down a street and find that perfect restaurant? Have you ever had a sense that something bad was about to happen? What about when you fell in love? Did you know that person was the right one or did you review your checklist of an ideal mate?

Scientific evidence supports the gut feeling. It isn't your imagination or pizza with too many toppings. It's "the body has two brains" concept – one in the skull and one in the gut. These brains connect and share feelings and information.

Researchers gradually are learning more about the gut's brain, known as the enteric nervous system, enough that a new field of medicine, called neuro-gastroenterology, has sprung up around their inquiry.

The gut's brain is in the sheaths of tissue lining the esophagus, stomach, small intestine and colon. Considered a single entity, it is packed with neurons, neurotransmitters and proteins that pass messages – a complex circuitry that enables it to act independently, learn, remember and, as the saying goes, produce gut feelings. The brain in the gut plays a major role in human happiness and misery.[22]

KEEP IT REAL

We all think with our gut, whether we consciously know it or not. In communication situations we want to listen to someone who is real. We listen to the person who our gut tells us is believable, honest and authentic. We measure the stories that they tell and decide with our gut if they have value. This is why we have to keep it real with the audience. They can tell if we are putting on an act or lying to them. If you have a problem with nervousness, take extra time to prepare. Also, see the next chapter for helpful ideas on that subject. Once we lose their trust, we may never get another chance.

Jesus had guts and chutzpah, which is the Yiddish word for "boldness, gall, audacity, and brazen nerve."[23] Jesus was thoroughly authentic in all that he did and said. Because of that he gave others permission to discover who they were. Multi-track communication touches us on levels that are difficult to verbalize. It is hard to give words to explain the "sense of knowing" because knowing just "is." How can you explain the thoughts that come from a place deep in your core that are ancient yet vibrate like the cries of a newborn?

So what does our Gut learn from the Prodigal story? If we are bold enough to look at ourselves truthfully, we discover that the

---

[22] *The New York Times, Human Body's Two Brain Work Together, Omaha World-Herald,* January 23, 1996 page 1.
[23] Page 123, *Jewish New Testament Commentary.*

prodigal's journey is our own. We want the best for ourselves so at the gut level we want the best outcome for the prodigal.

We can feel his pride, understand his arrogance. We know what he deserves for his stupidity, but we all secretly hope for better. We all hope for grace, and a second, third or fourth chance.

We all long for the father to run across the field to greet us. We pray to find forgiveness and tenderness. When we see him, the sight of his face and the sound of our name on his lips feels overwhelming. The love and longing in his eyes is too much to bear. Can we look at him, or does the weight of shame push our head down?

Do we hear the prodigal wonder? Why did I wait so long? Why did I suffer so long in a foreign land when my father loves me so? I have returned with hope and have been reborn into the land of the living!

SEEKING THE SPIRIT OF TRUTH

WHAT HAPPENED AFTER THE PARTY?

Jesus gave three distinct characters and plotlines in the story of the Prodigal. Of the three stories, it is the older brother's story that is left open ended. Jesus does not tell us what happens to him and how things went after the big party was over. What about the older brother?

As the first born in my family, it is easy to understand what the older brother might have felt. It's not fair when a younger sibling gets to play around while you have to fix dinner or clean the house. It is easy to understand how the older brother might have felt slighted and offended. They started the party without him for Pete's sake! Here is a mental dialogue the older bro might have had if he lived in Texas. Let's call him Oscar.

THOUGHTS FROM OSCAR, THE STAY-AT-HOME OLDER BROTHER, OF PRODIGAL FAME

Just a minute…who came back? Dad is doing what? How come no

one told me? This is too much. How can brother Zeek have the nerve to come waltzing back here like nothing happened? He has broken every law, every rule of my father. How dare he!

Makes me so mad! I have been breaking my back pulling rocks and digging fence posts for miles and miles. Yeah, the place has a great view and it's looking great because of my blood, sweat and tears. Why should I share that with this bum?

I have done everything right. I have worked like a slave – plowed, planted, harvested, sweat, run cattle in the freezing rain. Dad worked all his life to build a major ranching operation, when Zeek-man decided that he wanted his inheritance now...it messed everything up – cut us short on cash. But Dad went and liquidated half the operation and knocked us out of the control of the valley. Brother dearest has no idea how hard I have been working to regain the ground that we lost when he decided to pursue that stupid investment idea – and become a movie producer. Right. What a joke. Zeek is such a loser when it comes to business.

We all knew it was a mistake, but Mr. Know-it-all had to have his way. I knew when he started hanging out with those party animal friends of his; it was like graffiti on railroad cars, you could see it coming for miles. And then we get all those stories about auditions with showgirls in Vegas, yeah right! Talk about working for a living, how much did those parties cost him? Does he realize the embarrassment he has been to the family? He has shamed us.

Yeah, we had great times before he left. I can't believe that he had the nerve to show his face after blowing it big time! It nearly broke Dad's heart to see him leave. Dad sure has missed him. I saw how he would always go by his picture and touch it and sigh. For a tough man, he sure had a lot of tears in his eyes. He didn't think I noticed but, when he took his evening walks, he always used that walking stick that Zeek made for him. I know he was praying with every step.

Somehow Dad never gave up hope. He was always listening for the phone call, hunting through the mail and looking up when a foreign car came down the road. I can't believe he still loves him after all the trouble he has caused.

Now after an apology, Dad wants to throw Zeek a party. Unbelievable! Why hasn't he thrown a party for me? We're in the middle of the harvest and Dad stops everything for a fish fry and barbeque. How come I never got the royal treatment like the loser boy?? What are you telling me about that calf I had been hand feeding and prepping for some great t-bones? Dad has it on the grill? Why wasn't I asked first? Hey, I had plans for that heifer!

Jesus told this story for both the crowd and the religious leaders. The crowd needed to learn about a father's forgiveness. The older brother's conflict was a message to the religious about their attitudes and unwillingness to receive those whom the Father loved. As in many of his stories, Jesus left the ending of the story up to the listener. He did make it clear that there was a way home. One of the major challenges he had with the establishment was that they were acting instead of living truth. He challenged them to be congruent and to live the spirit of truth.

Religion, which has no practical impact on our daily lives, quickly becomes a vague, abstract notion that amounts to nothing. Many have nothing more than an empty profession to prove they are Christians. They are like the cinnamon tree whose outer bark is more valuable than all else that remains.

– William Gurnall [24]

SUMMARY

Have you ever tried to pour water into a bottle from a bucket? It is not an easy task and most of the water ends up on the floor instead of in the bottle. But, if you use a funnel it makes the task easier. People are like bottles. They have very narrow openings to pour information into. Multi-track communication gives you a funnel that helps you get your message into people. Multi-track communication is like multi-tasking with your communication signals.

[24] Gurnall, William *The Christian in Complete Armor, Devotional,* Edited by Moody Publishers, May 23.

Multi-track communication is more successful because it gives us more ways to connect with people. For example, if I have your home phone, cell phone, address, fax and email address, it is much easier to interact with you. Multi-track communication helps us to connect with people, physically, mentally, emotionally, intuitively and spiritually. This also helps us to create messages that stick like Mental Velcro in people's minds.

Master Communicators know how to maximize the impact of their messages by communicating simultaneously on many levels. When we use multi-track communication it is like having all the instruments in an orchestra play the same note. The unity creates a vibration that touches every part of the listener. Jesus was a consistent multi-track communicator. When we make a new connection, it helps us to reconnect to ourselves and to others.

Remember, you may only have one chance to plant a seed. So give it your best shot. Use all your tools and abilities to connect. Don't waste the seed of your life.

CHAPTER 7
PREPARATION – WEAVING THE NET

In the S.I.M.P.L.E.™ communication techniques of Jesus, "P" stands for Preparation. Master Communicators know that preparation is critical to success. It may take only a few hours to craft a Gettysburg Address, but it takes a lifetime to prepare the craftsman. To communicate effectively requires preparation in many areas, such as physical, emotional, intellectual and spiritual. Jesus prepared all his life for short years of ministry. As a leader he prepared others to follow after him. His preparation and discipline established the platform from which he launched history's most transformational marketing campaign.

I would rather see a sermon than to hear one any day;
I would rather one should walk with me than merely tell
the way.
The eye's a better pupil and more willing than the ear,
Fine council may be confusing, but example's always clear.
For I might misunderstand you and the high advice you give,
But there's no misunderstanding of how you act and how
you live.
– Edgar A. Guest, *Sermons We See*, 1881

DOING THE "RIGHT THING"

We have all heard and know why preparation is important but there is a huge gap between knowing and doing what needs to be done. On a personal level we all "know" that exercise and eating right is important. But what percentage of the time do we put on the jogging shoes or avoid those seductive French fries and comforting late night snacks? On a career level, we know that college, classes and accreditation is critical for professional success, but do we take the time to sign up for the training or complete the course work? On an achievement level it is easy to dream big dreams and write down goals, but what happens the day after tomorrow?

Preparation is a behavior pattern that lays the foundation for future success. Athletes and politicians understand this deeply. We love watching our favorites win and share the pain when they lose. The Olympics games remind us that the training of a lifetime and winning the gold is reduced to a fraction of a second.

So how do we prepare to be successful communicators in a microwave world? The question is, do you want to be the grasshopper or the ant? Grasshoppers are reactionary but they do get lots of exercise from jumping around dodging bullets. Ants have an organized approach and system for handling crisis. Ants are prepared for changes. Grasshoppers are victims of their behavior and die when the weather becomes harsh.

The bottom line is communication rules have changed with the Information Age. Before this when events occurred, politicians and business owners took time to craft their responses. Press conferences were more formal and people were better behaved, for the most part. Now the competition has created a media rat race over the same stories. And technology only increases the number of virtual eyeballs. We have reporters phoning in reports from cell phones. There are cameras small enough to attach to a reporter's glasses. Soon reporters won't need a satellite truck to go to a location because they will be able to plug into the phone jacks or electrical outlet to send the interview to the studio. This brings us to a time when plug and play will have a whole new meaning.

As news viewers, we have seen the consequences of lack of preparation during disasters and with Big Story surprises. The telltale signs are all the same: deer-caught-in-headlights look, quavering weak voice, angry words (retracted and apologized for later), slumped posture and stuttering excuses. Being caught in the cross-hairs of the media is not an easy place to be. An angry word, a lie or an inappropriate hug can fly around the world in seconds. For those in the public service, politics, high-profile businesses, or jobs dependent on media coverage, the best advice is, "Better safe than sorry!" Even if a crisis does not occur on your watch, it is much better to be prepared than to face the consequences – repeated lies, loss of public image or advertiser loyalty, or a drop in stock prices.

The next question is, will you be ready? As we say in media training, "When crisis knocks on your door, the TV Live truck will be there to help you answer."

BEING YOUR BEST REQUIRES PREPARATION

Being your best does not happen by accident. Even if you never expect to be in a news conference, there are thousands of other communication venues that require preparation. Whether it is a business presentation, press conference, luncheon speech, news interview or teaching a class on fishing, effective communicators prepare. Proper preparation requires a clear understanding of the mission, which forms the blueprint for action. Planning helps evaluate the goals, measure the audience, assemble and write, make the checklist and chart the map to success. The bigger an opportunity may be, the greater the amount of preparation.

As a media coach there are specific exercises and drills that I take my clients through. But the preparation varies because the presentation style and skills needed for a network news interview are vastly different than those required for a humorous after-dinner speech. The great news is that preparation pays off! Research shows that presentation jitters and nervousness can be reduced up to 70% by simply rehearsing and practicing ahead of time. The more we practice, rehearse and exercise our communication skills, the more confidence we have which builds our communication momentum.

HOW DID JESUS PREPARE FOR HIS MISSION AND LIFE?

Jesus was physically prepared for his life and call. The teachings, sermons, questions, schedule and impact demonstrate that he was thoroughly and deeply prepared. He was prepared physically, emotionally, intellectually and spiritually. Like all great leaders, Jesus prepared his disciples so that they would be successful. Let's begin with an area that seems obvious but is often overlooked.

PHYSICAL PREPARATION

During his public ministry, Jesus only traveled within a 50-mile radius of his home. Even though many of us drive that far for a good restaurant, we forget that Jesus walked everywhere in a world without running water, fast food and hotels. They depended on the hospitality of others for their daily bread and rest. There are several mentions of Jesus being exhausted, tired and weary from traveling and teaching. He was resting when he met the Samaritan woman at Jacob's well. Another time Jesus fell asleep in a boat, and even the winds and storm didn't wake him.

Being in the public eye is physically demanding. The time, the crowds, the emotions, the needs, rushed (if any) meals and sleep deprivation. With all our modern conveniences, it is easy to forget how different the conditions were in Jesus' time. Taking a trip to a third world nation gives us an idea. A friend of mine returned from a trip to orphanages in Africa where they were glad to drive almost four hours for a shower.

Being trained as a carpenter or builder must have contributed to Jesus' physical preparation. Like all Jewish boys, Jesus was trained in his father's trade. Joseph was a carpenter. In the Western mindset, carpentry is a wood worker. But the definition of a carpenter in Greek includes wood working and stone masonry with engineering abilities. A stonemason was a high-end tradesman and very much in demand in the two areas where Jesus grew up.

After Jesus' birth, Joseph took the family to Egypt and later moved to Nazareth. Nazareth was four miles from Sepphoris (modern Zippori) which became a major construction project of Herod Antipas (son of Herod the Great). This city was considered to be the most opulent city in Galilee and included a theatre that seated three thousand.[25] Considering the amount of reconstruction going on in the area, it may have been that Jesus was involved in a very profitable trade. Regardless of whether he was a raised as a carpenter or builder of stone, he was physically fit and probably very strong.

PHYSICAL DISCIPLINE OF FASTING

Jesus showed his strength and discipline when, after his baptism, he traveled into the wilderness to fast and pray for forty days without food. So why did Jesus fast? There is a mental clarity and spiritual sensitivity that comes from fasting. The brain spends the majority of its energy helping us digest food and when we allow it to rest from digestion, it is amazing how mental fog clears up. (Please note that fasting is not healthy for all individuals, especially those with health conditions, children or pregnant women.) But, there is a great difference in simple food or juice fasting to what Jesus did. To fast for forty days and nights meant that Jesus was one incredibly strong man. I know very few people who could meet the extreme demand of desert, wilderness and no food. This type of fasting builds an internal discipline and undoubtedly strengthened Christ's resolve when he faced future opposition.

A STORY TO REMEMBER

All great camping trips have a story to remember, and Jesus' was no different. Most stories are about getting lost in the woods, eating raw food, stepping on a slug barefoot or having a skunk spray the dog. At the very end of Jesus' Bootcamp, that's when the "evil alien" arrives. This bad dude fills the valley with the scent of fresh bread. "Hey Jesus, take a bite. Is that thunder I hear, or is it your

---

[25] Page 1638, Sepphoris, *Archaeological Study Bible*, *NIV*, Zondervan, Grand Rapids Michigan, 2005, page 1638, Sepphoris.

stomach rumbling?" Unimpressed with the evil alien's baking skills, Jesus leaves the restaurant. So the evil alien takes Jesus on a wild ride past the Las Vegas jackpots offering to make him full partner. Jesus declines the franchise. Then the evil one sweeps Jesus to the top of the UN building and offers him half of Manhattan if he will do the Spiderman jump off the side. Jesus takes a pass as he's seen the movie. The evil alien flies away and immediately fires his speech-writer and consultants. Jesus finds himself back at the campsite where angels were serving dinner.

There are some important communication principles that we all need to remember from Jesus' encounter with Satan (Matthew 4:1–11). First of all, Bad Guys have great timing. Their great timing is usually bad timing for you. The toughest test came when Jesus was exhausted and at his weakest physically. As the story goes, when Satan tempted him with doubt, wealth and the power of all kingdoms, Jesus did not waste energy arguing. Second point was that regardless of the distraction, Jesus, "stayed on message" and resisted the tempting offers. The result, faced with facts he could not conquer, the evil alien or Satan left.

APPLICATION

When dealing with situations or people who want to pull you off track, keep the focus, don't argue, and use the tool of truth. Remember that like lifting weights, resistance can assist you to reach higher goals.

For the same reasons, monitor your communication situations when you are tired. This may seem obvious, but unnecessary problems occur because tired people say stupid things. Don't get trapped. Slow down your word rate to avoid verbal blunders.

Definitely avoid confrontations and meetings with difficult people when you aren't up to it. It is easy to say the wrong thing that could cost you a client, a job or a relationship. When you know that it might be a demanding day at the office or on the road, prepare like an athlete. Eat the right foods, stay hydrated, take your vitamins, get enough rest and pace yourself.

WE LOVE WATCHING OTHERS PREPARE AND CHANGE

Interesting phenomena in reality television are shows like *Biggest Loser* and makeover programs. They reaffirm our desire to prepare and to exercise discipline. These shows help the audience live vicariously through challenges faced by overweight people who compete for the gold by learning to workout and change their eating habits. They learn new habits, disciplines and prepare themselves for a new and healthier life. The main challenge for the audience members who want to make similar changes is remembering that television compresses time and telescopes it down. As with any project, personal or business, it is important to properly and realistically measure the "Time on Task" needed to accomplish the goal.

Well, knowledge is a fine thing, and mother Eve thought so; but she smarted so severely for hers, that most of her daughters have been afraid of it since. – Abigail Adams

INTELLECTUAL AND EDUCATIONAL PREPARATION

Jesus grew up in the small farming town of Nazareth, which only had a population of around 500, but it was located next to Sepphoris, which was the capital of Galilee until A.D. 20.[26] Even though he grew up in a small town, the training and career paths for Hebrew boys was very structured. Only the best of the best became rabbis or teachers.[27] Memorization is an essential part of oral tradition. The ability to memorize and discuss huge volumes of material determined the educational progress and societal status of a man. Today, in traditional and orthodox schools this is still a critical part of the educational process.

In Jesus' time the average twelve-year old male was required to memorize the Penatuke or first five books of the Old Testament while learning the family trade. A few of the outstanding students sought permission to study with a rabbi for an extended period of time. These students were called talmidim (tamids), which means

[26] Page 1623, Nazareth, *Archaeological Study Bible*.
[27] Ray Vander Lann, *Rabbi and Talmidim*, article www.Followtherabbi.com. Acknowledgement also goes to the Vander Laan DVD series, In His Steps, Produced by Focus on the Family, Colorado Springs, Co. These are excellent resources and historical material.

disciple. If the young man had the ability to answer the questions (testing) of the rabbi, then he would leave his home to live and study with the rabbi. If a young man did not find a rabbi who would take him as a student, then he would return to his home and continue the family trade and marry when he was in his early 20's or younger.

For the young men who were accepted as disciple (talmid), they spent every waking moment, night and day with the rabbi. "There is much more to a talmid than what we call student." Ray Vander Laan explains, "A talmid wants to be like the teacher, that is to become what the teacher is. That meant that students were passionately devoted to their rabbi and noted everything he did or said."

A disciple was radically committed to his rabbi. They desired to be like him, to know how he prayed and to model his life. They spent every moment, night and day with the rabbi until they completed the next level of training in their late teens. During this time a candidate memorized the rest of the Old Testament. Becoming a disciple meant that all sorts of opportunities and privileges opened up to the chosen ones.

Women memorized the Psalms, the Proverbs and married at the onset of menses. Men usually married at the age of 18, but if they completed a higher level of academic training, they could delay marriage to the age of 30. Vander Laan and other scholars believe that Jesus had taken this course, which is why he was unmarried when he began his public ministry.

When Jesus called Peter, Andrew, James, John and the other disciples who were working at the family trade to follow him, no wonder they ran. They had been passed over and thought that they didn't have what it took to make it, mentally, spiritually or financially. When Jesus called them, the disciples got a second chance to study with a rabbi and have an opportunity to build a future. It was like someone walked up and gave them a free college scholarship without an entrance exam. Following a rabbi such as Jesus meant a man was more highly educated and could attain higher position, income, social standing and more.

APPLICATION

It is important to organize your thoughts before important communication opportunities. Even the best ad-libber is better with rehearsal. Besides, if you only have one chance to make a good impression, why leave it to chance? After you have thought through your answers or presentation, it is important to practice out loud.

The clearer the message, the more successful people are at staying on message during interviews, press conferences, and especially crisis communication situations. In high-risk conditions, be prepared, tell the story, keep to the facts, reinforce position and don't let reporters pull you off track with speculation or opinion (unless you are fully qualified to have one and are prepared for the onslaught).

When dealing with the media twenty years ago, the rule was, "Never complain, and never explain." While this may have worked for some corporate executives and Henry Ford a century ago, stonewalling can be a career-ending move. In other situations, it can be brilliant. Key to this concept is the importance of knowing with whom and when to share information. Remember the media needs facts, opinions or personal stories for a news story. If you have a great story that explains an issue or touches the heart it is important to be ready to share it on camera.

The challenge is if you don't give enough information on a big story, the media will speculate and fill in the blanks. Then you have to dig out from under another layer of information that may be misinformation. If you find yourself in the midst of a media firestorm, use advisors. Don't leak information to the troops unless you want the press to know it. Remember to have your facts, information and ducks in a row when involved in critical communication situations.

PREPARING THE HEART

But he did not commit himself to them, for he knew what people are like – that is, he didn't need anyone to inform him about a person, because he knew what was in a person's heart.
– John 2: 24–25, *Complete Jewish Bible*

Even though you respect and love people does not mean you trust them with all of your plans. There is a government and military term, "need to know basis," which means that people are given the information that is essential for completing the job. Just because you trust a solider does not mean that they get the codes for the missile launch sequences.

Jesus did not trust himself to any man because he knew how conflicted our hearts can be. Jesus loved his pupils, but knew that they were not mature enough to comprehend the scope of the job he had to do. Even his disciples continually misunderstood his actions and teachings. This is the challenge that comes with leadership and doing what is right. The resistance comes in like a flood, but in order to navigate the river a sailor has to keep a steady hand upon the rudder.

Jesus knew that his destiny required unconventional actions. He knew that these would be misunderstood. A parent says, "Trust me. You'll understand someday." Did Jesus trust them? Yes, he trusted them with his message but not with his plans.

There is a wise practice that military officers understand is critical to survival. Officers and soldiers should not socialize. It is counter productive on the battlefield. Like an officer leading his men into combat, Jesus knew he would have to do things they couldn't understand from the trenches. To help protect them from confusion and him from distraction, Jesus did not seek the approval or support of his followers.

The next chapter on Love discusses Jesus' love for his disciples and for his friends. He loved them dearly but knew his trial and death would confuse them. It might even cause them to turn away from their beliefs for a short time. Jesus knew the master plan. He knew they would return with greater commitment.

PROTECT YOUR DREAMS AND PLANS

A friend once told me that she learned to protect her dreams like a baby in the womb. Until it was time for the child to be born she would not speak of her dreams to anyone. Likewise, the great writer, Tennessee Williams would never talk about a book or play until it was finished.

Dreams and visions are birthed in our heart, which is why it is important to know whom and when you can trust with your dreams, especially when you are a leader. Jesus did not share the mystery of his plans with his disciples to protect them and to protect Himself.

It is also important to prepare our hearts when people fail the group and us. When people make mistakes and lose sight of a goal, it is important to push aside disappointment and not take their failure as being directed at us. Jesus knew that his followers would all be gripped with fear and jump ship during his trial, yet he didn't let that distract him from his goal or abandon his commitment to them.

In the same manner, when we have an employee or person who leaves a company, project or fellowship, it is important to keep focus and not take it personally. Dealing with an intentional betrayal is different than a foolish decision. Exercising greater love and pushing beyond the mistakes allows others to receive the same measure of grace and forgiveness we would hope to receive.

APPLICATION

Prepare and protect your heart when you are in difficult communication situations. Boundaries are important for protection on all levels.

EMOTIONAL AND CULTURAL PREPARATION

Emotional, relational and cultural intelligence are all interrelated. Jesus was an experienced communicator as shown by his ability to engage and connect with people from every realm of society. As discussed in the previous sections, his biblical grounding and spirited answers astonished people from every influential group – political, religious, financial, social, military and legal. Jesus unraveled their arguments and provided a clear path for truth.

As previously pointed out, Jesus' communication style was Eastern in thought and approach. It was not based on Western (Greek–European–American) thinking. Jesus used stories, examples, questions, props and riddles that had spectacular reach. Some were poetic, *"Consider the lilies how they grow; they toil not, they spin not; and yet I say unto you, that Solomon in all his glory was not arrayed like one of these.*[28] *Others were illustrations: "The kingdom of heaven is like a net which was thrown into the sea and gathered fish of every kind; when it was full, men drew it ashore and sat down and sorted the good into vessels but threw away the bad.*[29] *Others were mysterious: "I am the bread of life," "I am the door." "I am the vine."*

These examples show a deeper level of understanding how to communicate a message through story. He adds the next layer, which is wrapping the tale in the cultural setting of the listener. Jesus married simple cultural images with spiritual principles. This was the genius of his parables. Their use demonstrates that Jesus was prepared to effectively impart wisdom to any person of any culture. He followed the cultural rules and basic religious traditions as long as they were founded in God's instructions rather than man's interpretation. Jesus communicated clearly because he understood the culture and the people. His examples were simple enough to be understood by the youngest child and complex enough to baffle the leading scholars.

PREPARING THE SPIRIT

Prayer was mandatory, not optional, for Jesus. It was a lifestyle and the source of power, peace and passion. Prayer was the way Jesus connected to the Almighty. Through prayer he spiritually prepared Himself before any and every major decision, presentation or interaction. He knew that without a direct pipeline with the source of his strength he would quickly run out of steam. *Jesus said, "The Son can do nothing by Himself. He does only what he sees the Father doing, and in the same way."* – John 5: 19, *The Living New Testament.*

---

[28] Luke 12:27 King James Version.
[29] John 13:47 Revised Standard Version.

Here's a look at a few of Jesus' prayer times: before he started his ministry, before he chose his disciples, before he walked on water, before he healed the sick, before he raised the dead, before he fed the 5,000, and before he dealt with his trials. At every major junction, Jesus prayed and plugged into heaven.

The disciples noted that he got up early to pray. At the end of the day, he went off by himself to pray. The disciples recognized they needed to know the power of prayer. They asked him to teach them to pray. He taught them the words, "Our Father, who art in heaven." Jesus taught them to pray with love and not for power. Love unlocked the vaults of heaven.

APPLICATION

Jesus knew empowerment for his purpose came from going to his source. Going to our source spiritually empowers and prepares us for all that we do.

PREPARING OTHERS

THE POWER OF REHEARSAL

Jesus knew that he had to prepare his followers. They lived, walked, talked, watched, listened, and interacted with him wherever he went. Jesus knew that in order for his followers to master the material, they needed some serious field experience. This life course required practical application (on their own) before they could be trusted with the full weight of leadership. Just as you can't learn how to ride a bike by watching others, you have to get on the bike to learn how to ride.

The same principle is true for public speaking and verbal presentations. It takes practice to get it right. The more we practice the better we become and the more freedom we feel while presenting. Jesus practiced all the time. He taught all over Galilee. Like any teacher he used and developed stories as he went from town to town. The disciples must have heard them at different times and places, because the same stories appear in different places in the Bible.

The disciples traveled with Him and heard those teachings, day after day, week after week in town after town. They watched him teach, laugh, pray, bless and heal the crowds. By listening to him teach over and over, Jesus' disciples not only memorized the messages, but they began to live them. The best messages are those which people live.

After a year of watching him, Jesus sent pairs of his disciples on short sojurns as advance teams to the next village he would visit. Then after they were ready, Jesus sent them out on their own in pairs. After great success, the disciples returned and reported what had happened. Like a good general, Jesus debriefed the troops, handed out critiques and shouted out atta'boys.

APPLICATION

Jesus practiced teaching and fully prepared those he trained. After they watched and followed long enough, he then sent them out to practice. When developing and training others, give them time to listen and absorb what needs to be taught. Then when they are ready it is important to let them practice often. Constructive feedback is important to help people grow more quickly.

PREPARING OTHERS FOR THE BEST AND THE WORST

It is important to be honest with people about all the aspects of a job, especially when it might be a difficult one. Dropouts occur most amongst people who come to a job with unrealistic expectations. When the ups and downs occur and things get rough, like a plant without water, their enthusiasm turns into bitterness and complaining.

Honesty is the best policy when it comes to preparation. Jesus honestly told his disciples that they would face rejection, but not to let it affect them. *"If anyone will not welcome you or listen to your words, shake the dust off your feet when you leave that house or town."* (Matthew 10: 14, *HCSB*). Jesus told them not to worry about a closed door or closed heart, but to keep moving.

Jesus reminded them during the good times, when they enjoyed the benefits of popularity, to stay balanced, chill out and not let it go to their heads. He told them to expect hate, persecution, and false accusations and to not be naive. "Look I am sending you out as sheep among wolves. Therefore be shrewd as serpents and gentle as doves." Jesus also warned his followers that they would have a special kind of help in difficult times. *"But when they hand you over, don't worry about how or what to speak. For you will be given what to say at that hour, because you are not speaking, but the Spirit of your Father is speaking through you.* – Matthew 10: 16, 19–20, *HCSB*.

PREPARING FOR CHANGE

Businesses know that organizations do not do well with sudden changes. Sudden changes can paralyze a system, an airline, or an engine. The same applies to many other areas. To thrive and survive change requires preparation. Companies use experts in change management to prepare their staff to handle fluxes in the market. Communities stage disaster drills to practice for potential problems.

On critical topics, Jesus prepped the disciples using examples of faith. Most importantly he prepared the disciples for his death and resurrection. Throughout the last six months of his ministry, Jesus repeatedly told the disciples what lie ahead. He used both images and details. They were so focused on their agenda of routing out the Romans and making Jesus a king, they missed the preparation for his death. They didn't really comprehend his meaning until later.

Jesus' methods of preparation proved to be good. Even the preparation that his trainees couldn't hear, they understood later. These methods of preparation included: giving people an experience they could touch, feel, smell, even feel or fear. The best way to prepare people is to give them something they can walk through and personally experience. It's like having warm-up innings before the ball game.

When it came to prepping for his D-day, Jesus gave the disciples an experience they would never forget. He raised Lazarus or Eliezar, the Hebrew name, to life after four days in the tomb. In the next chapter, the Eliezar (Lazarus) account is played out from his POV. The Master Communicator demonstrated the power of God and prepared the trainees for his resurrection when Lazarus rose from the dead.

APPLICATION

When big changes appear on the horizon, prepare and inform your staff, company, clients or family. It will make the transition smoother. Repetition helps people transition through change. It's like the old public speaking rule: Tell 'em what you are going to tell them. Tell 'em what you're saying. Then tell 'em what you said.

PREPARE YE THE WAY

Like a voice of one crying out: Prepare the way of the Lord in the wilderness; make a straight highway for our God in the desert.
– Isaiah 40: 3, *HCSB*

No man is an island, even though some may try to buy one. Our way is made easier and path clearer by those who have plowed the field before us. Even Jesus had an advance man. John the Baptist was not your standard opening act. Everything about him was edgy, from his preaching to his appearance.

John knew his job. His passion broke up the hard ground of men's hearts. He used truth like a steamroller as he blazed the spiritual trail. John did not pull punches, especially regarding purpose. When others tried to stir up jealousy about Jesus, he shut them down. He explained the chain of command and that he was the opening act for the main event. Jesus deeply appreciated John's service and his devotion. When others gossiped and belittled John, Jesus responded by taking the high road, literally out of town.

"Can I carry your water?" is an old country expression that is a serious offer to help. Water is heavy, especially enough water to take care of livestock on a ranch. John did more than carry the water for Jesus; he brought the river of people to Jesus.

SOLOMON – ADVANTAGES OF GENERATIONAL PREPARATION

The name King Solomon creates immediate responses, images and lessons. History records his astonishing wealth, remarkable wisdom, writings, and many, many wives. Solomon was a progressive ruler and remarkable business entrepreneur. He established a model for supply chain economics. Solomon identified the best talent, then hired or partnered with them to build the manufacturing and distribution channels. Solomon brilliantly developed strategic business partnerships and then consummated them by marrying Big Daddy's daughters, sisters, and more daughters.

He co-ventured with the Phoenicians for shipping, building and manufacturing of copper and brass. He controlled the transportation industry by supplying his northern neighbors, the Syrians, with Egyptian chariots and horses from Turkey. Even the original Spice girl, showed up to get in on the action! Legend states that the Queen of Sheba, returned home with trade agreements, and many gifts from the king including a little Solomon in the basket.

Like his father, King David, Solomon was a prolific writer with hundreds of songs to his credit. His most legendary accomplishment was building his temple, which was the most spectacular and costly building project of its day. The front pillars with capitals almost 35' tall and 19' wide were decorated with 400 pomegranates hanging from bronze nets. Talk about a fruit basket!

There was a brass "Sea" for ceremonial washing, which was cast from one piece of metal and held 11,000 gallons of water at capacity. It measured 15 feet across and about 7 feet deep and was the size of a swimming pool. He completed the temple in seven years, which included gold plating, gold ornaments, ivory inlay, weavings, paintings and carvings by the best craftsmen of the time.

Even though Solomon's accomplishments stood out, he didn't get there on his own. King David was the visionary. David's sins kept him from building the temple. When he asked to start this building project, he heard the Almighty say "no." But he prepared for the project his son would build. He assembled materials and Solomon built it with a flair.

The Copper King

Legends and fables have referred to King Solomon's mines. Movies have painted these as gold mines, but Archeologist Professor Nelson Glueck believed that Solomon was the greatest exporter of copper in the ancient world.[30] The ancient town of Ezion-geber (on the Red Sea) was not only a great seaport controlled by Solomon but was a manufacturing center as well. In this desert area where the winds would sweep down the wadi, Glueck found casting molds, copper slag and a huge walled enclosure with bricked air passages. It seems that they used they used the incessant desert winds as bellows to compress air to create a huge blast furnace and forge. This system explains the ability of the craftsmen to create metal work of such enormous structure. So, Solomon even used nature in his preparations.

Solomon was the Rockefeller of his time. At the end of his life he measured and wrote, "Vanities of vanities, all is vanity … there is nothing new under the sun." He built a remarkable temple of worship that was the praise of all nations, but his own temple was barren. Was he depressed or peaceful as he sang, "Your face Lord, I seek?" With all the riches and inheritance that his father David provided, Solomon had forgotten the greatest blessing of all – a relationship with the Almighty. He prepared his building projects, but failed to prepare himself.

Summary

Today we enjoy resources everyday that only kings or emperors would have enjoyed 200 years ago. We all benefit and build upon the preparation of others. We have such freedoms that were

---

[30] Keller, Werner, *The Bible as History, A Confirmation of the Book of Books*, translated by William Neil, William Morrow and Company, New York, 1956; 15th printing revised by author 1964. Pages 195–197.

paid for by countless sacrifices of those who have gone before. They are called pioneers, leaders, way makers, martyrs, patriots, but we recognized them as parents, teachers, mentors, friends, soldiers, firemen, policemen, public servants and so many, many more. How blessed we are to walk in the footsteps of those who have prepared the way for us. It's important to pass it on and willingly prepare the way for others.

Preparation forms the foundation for successful communication. Like floor beams, preparation includes many areas: physical, educational, emotional, spiritual and generational. Jesus prepared his entire life for a short, but profoundly successful, service to the public. His preparation and discipline established the platform from which he launched history's most successful marketing campaign.

PROFILE
ELEAZAR'S STORY (LAZARUS)

The burning fever came on you so suddenly, Eleazer. You staggered and collapsed in the field. They carried you into the house like a child. As you laid on the pallet, you were awake, asleep; it was day; it was night. You felt cool rags on your head and heard your own moaning. You choked when they poured weak wine with bitter herbs down your throat. Your head felt as if it would explode. What would stop the pain?

The doctors brought potions, plasters and leeches. But you floated in and out of darkness, babbling and repeating the words, "Adonai Eloheim."

You heard voices sometimes close, sometimes far. Marta sent for Yeshua to come. So why do your sisters, Miriam and Marta, both look so worried? You pat Miriam's cheek tenderly, and say, "Yeshua said he would see us before Passover, trust him."

Another day. You feel groggy and unable to focus. Your head tilts back as water is poured into your mouth. You can barely swallow. The pain causes you to stir. Voices say, "Miriam, there is nothing else we can do. He is dying."

"Yeshua is coming, Marta. All will be well," Miriam says defiantly. She holds your hand. "Don't die, brother. The Master comes. He comes quickly." With all your strength you smile, and pat her hand, "I know."

As the darkness overtakes you, Yeshua's warm, familiar voice sounds near. *Is he here? Am I imagining him?*

He sounds distant, but still it is his voice. "Eleazer, do you trust me?"

You feel the peace and commitment of deep, abiding friendship. You trust him absolutely. "Yes, Lord, I trust you with my life."

You feel so tired. Sleep comes now – deep, deeper like ascending a long, narrow pit, further and further down. Miriam prays every psalm that she knows, over and over, until her voice has faded into a hoarse whisper.

In your mind, you see the face of Yeshua the day he worked beside you in the vineyard, adding his strength to the harvest. "Eleazer," he asked, "do you love me?"

"Yes Lord, I love you with my all my spirit, soul and strength." His image fades from your memory. The pain finally drains. Your body seems to float now.

Drifting away, Miriam drapes herself over your chest. Her body shakes with sobs. "Brother, don't go, don't go." With a final breath, you say, "Trust him." The pain leaves completely. More darkness.

You feel suspended in utter darkness – outer darkness. A flash of lightning hits the cold ground beside you. It's cold, so, so cold – and dark – utterly black. Shock waves rock your feelingless corpse and awareness grows. The loud clap of thunder sounds deafening. You feel confused. What? The walls around you echo your name, "Eleazer!" The Master calls, "Eleazer, come out!"

---

[31] Page 191, *Jewish New Testament Commentary.*

Now your arms and legs tingle, but you cannot move. *Something binding. What is it? Why am I wrapped so tight? I can barely breathe. Whew! That awful smell – and the perfume.*

"Eliezar, come out!"

Okay, I'm trying. Where am I anyway? It's pitch black. This doesn't look like my room. Oh no, this is the tomb. They put me in the tomb. They must have thought I was dead and buried me. Maybe I was dead. Did I die? *"Eliezar!"*

With your legs somewhat bound, you shuffle from the tomb and into the blinding afternoon sun. A crowd applauds and cheers.

(Eliezar, Marta and Miriam are the Hebrew names for Lazarus, Martha and Mary. See John 11: 1–43.)

So Caiaphas, the high priest, told ruling council to get a grip and look at the options. He reminded them that it was better for one man to die than for the entire nation to perish. Considering how many Jews had been killed by Rome, this seemed like a win–win for the nation and the council, but a definite no-win for Jesus. So the plan was agreed to, all present signed off, made assignments and began building the case against Jesus. See Ch. 11 Dealing with Communication Difficulties and how Pilate dealt with a media crisis.

CHAPTER 8
LOVE – LIGHTING THE WAY

Love is the greatest of all emotions. Songs have been sung, countless battles won and quests for love begun. It is the fifth characteristic of the S.I.M.P.L.E.™ Method of communication. Love is the fuel, passion, commitment and reason that a person gets up before the sun rises to go "fishing." Jesus taught, spoke, modeled and lived love so that it made his communication life-giving.

If I speak with human eloquence and angelic ecstasy but don't love, I'm nothing but the creaking of a rusty gate.

If I speak God's Word with power, revealing all his mysteries and making everything plain as day, and if I have faith that says to a mountain, "Jump," and it jumps, but I don't love, I'm nothing.

If I give everything I own to the poor and even go to the stake to be burned as a martyr, but I don't love, I've gotten nowhere. So, no matter what I say, what I believe, and what I do, I'm bankrupt without love.

– 1 Corinthians 13: 1–3, THE MESSAGE

Love is the heart and core of communication. It is impossible to build a marriage, family, community, church or launch a mission, or dream without love. Love is what makes a person get out of bed with joy. Love is the glue between relationships and the fuel that makes the words "for better or worse, in sickness and in health – till death do us part" real. All people are wired to be part of families. And it is only through communities that people are challenged to use their gifts and discover their purpose. And when a personal need exists, people are best healed in an environment of love.

"What is true love?" asks the child. "Will I ever find it?"

The grandfather shrugs and nods, *"Yes, but only if you have the courage to look into the mirror of truth and have the strength to listen to your heart."*

Master communicators help us discover love because they help us discover ourselves. They hold up a mirror of truth to our lives and help us to see the truth of our hearts. Years ago, during a time of growth I discovered that:

When the pure tune of heart flows freely out . . .
My spirit rejoices, while my eyes can do nothing but cry.
– Lynn Wilford Scarborough

How Do We Connect and Reconnect?

In a world of ultra-connectivity, it stands to reason that people would be more connected. But it seems that the faster we go, the more disconnected we become. Travel disconnects us from lovers, family and friends. Computers keep us connected to the virtual world often at the expense of interpersonal or community activities. Television provides extreme sporting activities and other entertainment – but at the cost of becoming personally disconnected from our bodies and from our health. Our eyes view hours of romance on the big screen but we find no personal love or tender touching.

In response to the needs of "Global Villagers," the media's many faces converge like a multi-tasking Super Yenta to dispense wisdom. Talk show hosts teach us how to talk to each other. Daytime shrinks shame guests so they learn how to build healthy relationships. Harry meets Sally and Sally emails Harry on the Internet. Satellite radio jocks shock and unite us with disgust. Books give road maps to healthy hearts and to hearty health.

Still people search for their core. Disconnection from each other is one of the greatest challenges of our age. Master Communicators are in the business of connecting and reconnecting people with their hearts, bodies, spirits, children and abilities. They use "Multi-track" messages, which successfully resonate and are memorable. Master Communicators are also successful because they are "loving," which means they offer solutions that meet the needs of others.

MANY WORDS FOR LOVE

Love is the will to extend oneself for the purpose of nurturing one's own or another's spiritual growth. – M. Scott Peck, M.D.

The English word "love" has many meanings and interpretations. The Greeks had three words for love: Eros – romantic love between couples; Philos – brotherly love; and Agape – the highest form of spiritual or divine love. In the Old Testament is found ahavah (love) and chesed ("loving-kindness"). In this chapter and book, the word love refers to either to PHILOS, or the love between friends and family, and AGAPE, describing the quality love between the Creator and mankind.

Love is more than a software program we upload on demand. The need for love has been hardwired into our internal circuitry. Unfortunately the complexities of life are constantly challenging both our software, which is our experiences, and our hardware, which represents our needs. Both systems break down. Loving communication can get them up and running again.

WHERE DO WE SEE TRUE LOVE?

We have been programmed to watch and see love in dramas, comedies and tragedies. But as we watch the stage of our lives, imposters appear in rich costumes with masks. Guilt, lust, manipulation, envy or flattery can look like love. Time and consequences eventually peel away the masks of deception.

Sometimes respected leaders and admired individuals communicate in negative ways that can be destructive to us. We can exercise care in what we hear by measuring the nature of the message. No matter the source, it's important to recognize if the interactions sound laden with falsehood, games, and malice. If they do, take control. Take action. Turn off the TV. Leave the movie. Leave the house. Exit the harmful conversation.

> *The best place to find God is in a garden. You can dig for him there.*
> – George Bernard Shaw

IN THE BEGINNING – GARDEN GAMES

Do you ever have problems communicating? Most of us do. If you aren't aware of any, perhaps you live in a cave, or you are extremely privileged. Or are you in major denial? Or is it everyone else who has all the problems? Communication problems started in the Garden of Eden.

In the great dramatic opening scene of all time, the disconnects and accusations we experience today are all there – shame, blame, guilt, lies, spin, silence and twisted messages. Eve talks to the snake. The snake lies and twists the truth.

You may wonder, why was she hanging out with a snake? Was Adam not much of a talker? Was he present at the time? If so, why didn't Adam speak up and try to control the snake's spin?

Anyway, back to the plot line: Eve believes serpent-head's hype. He convinces her that she doesn't really have much sway with the Big Boss. She buys it. With fruit in hand, she tells her man, "C'mon, dear, everyone's doing it!"

Do you think Eve and the snake double-teamed Adam about the issue? If so, then wouldn't you expect a flag on that play?

Adam eats. They soon discover the snake lied and there is a "no return" policy on opened produce. The couple responds like "Ok, gotta go. And quick, let's cover things up and act like nothing happened."

Later that evening, the Boss shows up for a walk. "Hey, Adam where are you?" (Did God seek information? No, He knew what had happened, but did they? When God asks a question, it is for our benefit.)

So, Adam blames Eve. Eve blames the Snake. God knocks the snake's legs off. And the Big Angel with the Sword of Fire evicts everyone. Talk about a communication meltdown! Worse yet, we are still dealing with the consequences.

There are three common problems in any relationship between men and women – whether single or married – and they are communication, sex and money.
– Dr. Ed Cole[32]

THE MANY COLORS OF LOVE

There are many dimensions to love. When you hear the word "love" where does your mind go? Is love personal, such as caring, romance, touching or deep commitment? Is love on a social level, such as respect, compassion, honesty or giving to a cause?

Jesus embodied all of these characteristics and so many more. He walked, talked, taught and modeled love. While Shakespeare spoke of love and romance, Jesus lived the love of ages. He personified the divine romance. The impact of his love redefined everything – from marriage, to government, to every relationship and social institution.

LOVE MADE SIMPLE

In the same way, if you talk to a person in some language he doesn't understand, how will he know what you mean? You might as well be talking to an empty room. Living New Testament. – I *Corinthians* 14: 9

Jesus made love simple. He redefined love in terms that were easy to understand. When asked which of God's laws was most important, he answered.

Now the Pharisees heard that He had silenced the Sadducees, and so they had a meeting. And one of their number, an expert in the law, to tempt Him, asked, "What sort of command is greatest in the law?" And He answered him, "You must love the Lord your God with your whole heart, your whole soul, and your whole mind. This is the greatest command, and is first in importance. The second is like it: 'You must love your neighbor as you do yourself.' The essence of the whole law and the prophets is packed into these two commands."
– Matthew 22: 34–40, *Williams*[33]

[32] Dr. Edwin L. Cole, www.edcolelibrary.com, See Colisms for great life principles or for more help go to his book, *Communication, Sex and Money*, Watercolor Books, Southlake, TX.
[33] William – *New Testament in the Language of the People*, The Four Translation New Testament, Printed for Decision Magazine by Worldwide Publishing Minneapolis, MN, 1966.

What a brilliant synopsis! He took all of the "vitamins" threw them in the blender and came up with a life-giving smoothie mission statement. Just as the point of vitamins is to make us healthy, God's laws were given because they are good for us. But vitamins don't work if they are hidden in the kitchen cabinet. They work inside the human body.

Jesus' summary took everything back to the basics and reconnected all parts of man. With two simple sentences he "knocked the ball out of park with the bases loaded." He connected the law to love, the head to the heart, the spirit to the soul, God to man, man to man and man to himself. Love is the source that helps people to connect internally and externally in relationships and community.

LOVE HAS ROOTS

This sounds basic. Yet, a grip on the basic can be loosened or lost due to a fast paced schedule. When a politician changes focus and forgets the needs of his constituents, his next election may spell disaster. When a department store buyer loses touch with the latest trends, it's "clearance" time. How does Hollywood stay connected with relevant stories? One way writers and producers remain current is with recent stories "based on actual court cases." Jesus understood his roots and his audience. He wrapped his words around the listener with a warm blanket of relevance.

APPLICATION

Stay connected internally and with your roots. Why do you do what you do? What is your purpose? To whom are you responsible? For those in leadership and in the public arena, never forget "the ties that bind." Recognize the cement that holds you in position – your core audience. Remain aware of your message to them. Keep your ego in check. Exercise caution about believing flattery. Be careful about buying into what the media writes or says about you. Though it can be tough to hear truth, it is important to have co-workers, friends and family members who care enough to be honest. The alternative is losing those who will tell you the truth to those who care more for themselves and will be happy to discuss your shortcomings under the warm wash of neon lights.

Love your enemies for they will tell you your faults.

– Benjamin Franklin

CONNECTION – WHO IS MY NEIGHBOR?

Love is something that you can give everyday of your life.

Jesus loved everyone: young, old, rich, poor, privileged, uneducated, diseased, blind or unclean. Jesus' actions were counterculture in a world with layers of tradition, strict religious laws and deep religious prejudice. He loved not only with his words but also with his actions. The religious criticized him for hanging out with low-lifers. He issued a biting reply to this accusation.

While Jesus was having dinner at Matthew's house, many tax collectors and "sinners" came and ate with him and his disciples.

When the Pharisees saw this, they asked his disciples, "Why does your teacher eat with tax collectors and 'sinners'?" On hearing this, Jesus said, "It is not the healthy who need a doctor, but the sick. But go and learn what this means: 'I desire mercy, not sacrifice.' For I have not come to call the righteous, but sinners."

– Matthew 9: 10–13, *NIV*

Box Office Mysteries

Speaking of laws and commandments, for over two decades MovieGuide.org has tracked the box office success of movies in relationship to their values. Their research reveals that movies with strong, positive family/ faith and Judeo-Christian values make six to ten times more money at the box office than films fraught with violence, sex and adult language.[34]

---

[34] MovieGuide.org, Founder Dr. Ted Bahre. Movieguide is dedicated to redeeming the values of the mass media, by influencing entertainment industry executives and helping families make wise media choices.

Get the picture? To draw such a crowd, this must have been one great dinner party with one very interesting guest list. The food and music would have been amazing. Could the negative comments been flavored with jealousy? Hey Abe, did you notice the "Iron Chef" van pulling up in front of Matt's house?

How did Jesus respond to "Why do you hang out with such disgusting people?" His reply went something like this: "Get out of my face. You are clueless! You don't understand my mission statement. And it's been so long since you called home, that you've forgotten your own phone number."

Jesus said he came for those who wanted help. He came for the spiritually sick. He came for those who could be honest about their condition. He came for those who were willing to admit their state – the humble. My life's a mess, hey rabbi, can you spare some time?

The Pharisees and Sadducees revealed their thoughts of superiority through their words. They flaunted their spiritual "wellness" and arrogance. Unfortunately, personal pride made them unteachable. Thinking they "had it all together," unlike us sinners, cemented their hearts so they couldn't even hear Jesus. They refused to love. So despite their lofty positions, Jesus tossed them a bomb instead of a bone.

He challenged them with a concept about the focus of the Father's heart. Love and mercy, not sacrifice and rituals touch the Father. This core principle guided Jesus' steps. His actions demonstrated true love. He redefined "Who is my neighbor?" He expanded the community to outside the "hallowed" walls so that everyman became our neighbor. Jesus loved, touched and healed all, from the greatest to the least. He gave his best to all men.

APPLICATION

Who's my neighbor? Is he next door, at the office, at the store, in a house of worship, in the community? Is he checking into a hotel? Does he live in the city of the country? Are you a good neighbor – personally, locally and globally?

Try this on for size. Do you know the names of the people who live on your block – even if they don't have kids who attend school with your kids?

One wise Native American Chief said that they are taught to consider the impact on four future generations before making each decision for their tribe. If more individuals, leaders, teachers and company executives used a 4G (fourth-generation) perspective, how would our world change? Considering future generations adds a love perspective to whatever the problem might be.

Now think: "What are you doing to be a better neighbor? Is there anything your family could do to contribute to your community? Is there anything your company can re-invest in your local area, in future industry or the emerging world that would leave a legacy fueled by love and shaped by vision?

So in everything, do to others what you would have them do to you, for this sums up the Law and the Prophets. – Matthew 7: 12, *NIV*

WHAT'S YOUR HEART CONDITION?

Have you heard that symptoms of heart attack are different for men and women? That stems from a man's arteries being more likely to become blocked – or the pathways to his heart becoming more impass-able. Did Shakespeare call this a "hard heart?"

WE KNOW YOUR NAME
STARBUCKS SUCCESS 101
We all need community. Remember the theme song for the sitcom Cheers, "I want go to a place where everybody knows my name." – Scott Peck, M.D. gave this explana-tion:

In and through community lies the salvation of the world. Nothing is more important. Yet it's impossi-ble to describe community meaningfully to someone who has never experienced it – and most of us have never had the experience of true community.[35]

Everyone wants to belong and to be loved and appre-ciated. Whether we are at the office, home or place of faith, we need to include others. Everyone wants to go to a place where they are known, which is one of the reasons why Starbucks is so successful. When you walk in they are glad to see you. They say "Hi Joe-Bob, LaQuita, Catherine, Gwyneth or Jose" and shout out your name again when your drink is ready.

I enjoy walking in the mall with Starbucks employees. My friends Addi and Shannon see someone walk by and say, "That's a Venti Latte or Café Americano decaf." How strange that we now have coffee labels attached to us, but I guess it is better than being super-sized double meat, double cheese on a sesame bun.

[35] M. Scott Peck, M.D., *The Different Drum*, Simon and Schuster, New York, N.Y, 1987.

Heart disease in women often starts on the microscopic level, with a symptom called Vascular Dysfunction. The blood vessels supplying the heart don't expand properly to accommodate increased blood flow. It's almost as if the "heart breaks."

Even though a "hard heart" is very different than a "broken heart," women are less likely to survive a heart attack than men. No one says why – but one reason may be that the symptoms for women are subtler. Fortunately, for both men and women, making healthier choices in diet, exercise and smoking habits can reduce the chance of a heart attack.

This is more than an interesting fact; it is a scientific parable that reflects how different men's and women's heart responses are to emotional issues. The gender variation in heart disease is a reflection of the spiritual differences in reaction to stress and grief. In marital conflict, men are less willing to talk and tend to shut down. It's as if men have a "hard heart." Most women are more emotional and heart-driven, which makes them more vulnerable to victimization. Women love stories of romance novels. When women are stressed by relationship problems around them, it can strain their heart and lead to a broken heart.

Even though a heart may be in great physical condition, it may still be ill on other levels. Guard your heart for out of it flows the fountain of life, states the wisdom literature. Jesus taught that it was important that our hearts be connected to our heads, spirits and words. This is why he kept calling the religious ones, "Hypocrites." In Greek, the same root word translates "hypocrites" as "actors." This was like calling the high-brow religious ones, soap opera stars or theatrical play actors.

The Heart – Spirit Connection

Jesus was spiritual, but not religious. He lived in harmony with the law, but was not crushed by it. He lived in total freedom, yet walked in total obedience. He was simple and direct, but mysterious and unfathomable.

As explained earlier, Jesus and the simplicity of his message offended those who controlled the religious culture. The religious culture had become bound and controlled by thousands of laws upon rules upon laws. Like a 1,000-page tax document, it was impossible to follow, much less live by. The system had lost its true north and forgotten why God reached out to Abraham in the first place.

Jesus told them that they had put people into the bondage of man's rules instead of teaching and demonstrating to others the way of true faith and spirit. Jesus took them back to the basics. It was about relationship. It all started with the heart of the Father who reached out to the heart of man. As a relationship grows from the spirit and heart, so true faith must follow the same path. Jesus re-established this basic truth for the world and took it to a new dimension of intimacy.

The underlying question that he reminded them was, "Why?" Why gives a mirror that will tell us the truth if we are willing to look in it. Jesus told them that their heart had to be circumcised, which was a perplexing image used by the prophet Isaiah. Circumcision was more than a law given for health reasons; it was an outward sign of spiritual separation. Isaiah continually admonished people that their hearts were hard and unfeeling.

When Jesus used this term he implied several things. First, cut away our selfishness so that our true heart could be directed to the Father. Second was for man to strip away the religion and rules of man so that they could worship in spirit and truth.

Why would God care about our hearts so? Jesus taught that his mission was to reconnect people to their eternal father. All he had was his life and words to accomplish this mission. But his clarity, focus, discipline and love helped him to do that. Here are the words that he spoke that clearly defined his mission:

Then Jesus cried out, "The one who believed in Me believes not in Me, but in Him who sent Me. And the one who sees Me sees Him who sent Me. I have come as a light into the world, so that everyone who believes in Me would not remain in darkness. If anyone hears My words and doesn't keep them, I do not judge him; for I did not come to judge the world but to save the world. The one who rejects Me and doesn't accept My sayings has this as his judge: the word I have spoke will judge him on the last day. For I have not spoken on My own but the Father Himself who sent Me has given Me a commands to what I should say and what I should speak. I know that His command is eternal life. So the things that I speak, I speak Just as the Father has told Me. – John 12: 44–50, *HCSB*

Don't Be an Actor

Jesus pointed out that religious leaders who criticized him were "actors" who pretended to be spiritual. Jesus said they were like film extras who went through public displays of prayers and sacrificial acts rather than putting them into action. They acted like they had love in their hearts while they acted on the stage of pretension. We all hate being manipulated and put down by those who are snobby and self-important. Jesus pointed out the need for "spiritual heart surgery" with comments like:

A good man produces good out of the good storeroom of his heart. An evil man produces evil out of the evil storeroom, for his mouth speaks from the overflow of his heart. – Luke 6: 45, *HCSB*

It's not what goes into a man's mouth does not make him "unclean," but what comes out of his mouth, that is what makes him "unclean."
– Matthew 15: 11, *NIV*

Application

Check what's in your heart, especially if you are reaching out to others. Do you have a heart condition that needs to be resolved? Do you speak bitterness, anger, disappointment and pain? Check yourself for blind spots. Have you been acting lately? You might as well examine yourself. Discerning folks will see those blind spots whether you recognize them or not.

TURN THE OTHER CHEEK – THE POWER OF FORGIVENESS

"But I say to you who listen: love your enemies, do good to those who hate you, bless those who curse you, pray for those who mistreat you. If anyone hits you on the cheek, offer the other also.... Even sinners love those who love them.... Love your enemies, do what is good, and lend, expecting nothing in return. Then your reward will be great."
– Luke 6: 27–36, *HCBC*

Unforgiveness and bitterness destroy positive emotions and cause disconnection. Take some little rocks of offense, add some complaints, stir and within a week a fully baked wall of grudges pops out of the oven. Blend in a little more gossip; fold in some envy and your cake floats in a moat of bitterness, which surrounds the towering layers of righteous indignation. Toss some misunderstanding into the mix and watch the anger flare. Baked Alaska just burnt beyond recognition.

Once a strong tower of unforgiveness is erected, the only way to open it is from the inside out. To open the walled-off tower, we have to choose to open the door. Our will is the deadbolt lock. That's why Jesus recommended a new way of living – living with forgiveness.

"You have heard that it said, 'Love your neighbor, and hate your enemy.' But I tell you, Love your enemies, and pray for those who persecute you. In this way you will show you are sons of your Father in heaven."
– Matthew 5: 43–45, *Beck*

"You have heard it said an eye for an eye and a tooth for a tooth. But, I tell you, don't oppose an evil man. If anyone slaps you on your right cheek, turn the other cheek to him." – Matthew 5: 38–39, *Beck*

"If you forgive men when they sin against you, your heavenly Father will also forgive you." – Matthew 5: 14, *NIV*

Only perfect people don't need forgiveness. Forgiveness is something that we all need to give with grace. Forgiveness opens the doors and extends the welcome mat to others. As long as we walk in the world we will have dirty feet. We all need to ask forgiveness of those we've offended with sincerity.

When we drink the waters of bitterness and walk in the dirt of offenses, it makes our path a muddy mess. Remember what your mom said, "Don't walk inside with muddy shoes. I just mopped the kitchen floor!" We need to be careful not to carry the mud into our internal houses. So get the soap, cleanse your heart, scrub off the prickly prides, and wash in the waters of humility. To the Essene Jews, ritual bathing represented a cleansing from the world, sins, offenses and separation from the Almighty. The "Bathing" helped to receive forgiveness.

Without forgiveness the best of marriages fall apart and great companies unravel. Like a computer virus, bitterness infiltrates all parts and shuts down the operating system. Without forgiveness there is no hope or future. Forgiveness has to be a daily process of keeping the dirt and mud out of our houses. In the Lord's Prayer, Jesus taught people to request, "Forgive us our sins as we forgive others."

> *Love looks through a telescope; envy through a microscope.*
> – Josh Billings

AND THE MESSAGE IS …

Did you ever watch the show *Touched by an Angel?* In a *60 Minutes* interview, Executive Producer, Martha Williamson explained the show's focus. "If you look at it, we are dealing with the same issues on *Touched by an Angel* or *Promised Land* that *NYPD Blue* or *Law and Order* deal with. We just come from a very different point of view, which is God's point of view. And we have a message: 'God loves you. God exists.'" I recall that the late Ed Bradley asked Martha if there was a problem with that, to which she replied, "Not at all. God loves you, get over it."

In spite of the initial belief that a prime-time network show about God would fail, *Touched by an Angel* ratings soared until the final episode in April 2003. Episodes are still enjoyed today. The same simple message, God Loves You was one of the pivotal headlines that caused Jesus of Nazareth to passionately minister. It was a different point of view, a view from heaven that transcends time.

Jesus taught about connecting and reconnecting. When He taught about love, He gave people new eyes to see with, fresh words to speak, new values to bless others, a new path to walk and a new model to follow. He demonstrated love as the source of all that is done well. Jesus lived in the power and purpose of love.

No matter how many facts the brain may hold, it can never out weigh the truth that the heart believes. – Lynn Wilford Scarborough

JESUS BUILT A BRIDGE TO FATHER

Jesus taught with authority, asked questions with agility, told stories majestically, but when he spoke about the Almighty, he spoke about relationships. Jesus brought God close with terms such as My Father in Heaven or Abba. Abba means Daddy – an intimate, endearing term. Jesus' example connected men to the possibility of a relationship with the Source of Life itself.

Jesus connected us to heaven as if he placed a simple, direct, vertical phone call between man and the Almighty. No sales reps, no interest, no commissions, no bureaucrat, no lawyers – just you and Big Daddy. The new vocabulary along with his example built a bridge that carried men from slavery to beloved sons and daughters. When we love someone we want to be in relationship with him or her. The whole point of Jesus' life and mission was to tell people God loves them and wants a relationship with them. It all depends on your heart.

Would you reject a baby because of a dirty face and hands? No. You'd just say, "Time for a bath." What about when a child spills milk? Does that cause parents to discard their children? Of course not. Things like these do not threaten the relationship between

Passport for Supernatural

Jesus gave men an opportunity for a new passport – a citizenship that would allow them to pass into eternity with confidence. It was not a belief system with rituals to follow. This passport was an exchange for the supernatural life – accepting Him as the Son of Man and Son of God. His death paid the cost of wrong-doing and entrance into the God-life.

Like the tables of the moneychangers, he turned all the "proper" spiritual values upside down – faith not works, humility not pride, character not position, and sons not slaves. The standard contract was fairly simple – you gave him the debt, mistakes, inadequacies, sin and other junk and gave him your heart – you got

parent and child. Parents love their children. They take joy from their kids and understand that cleaning up messes is part of the job code.

Life is messy. We get dirty. Like dirt on the face of a child, sin didn't bother Jesus. He looked past it. He weighed the heart and if it was humble and soft soil, he planted a seed. He said, "Behold I am knocking on your front door." Plain and simple, he asked to come into the house. He didn't ask how it looked inside. He helped clean it up. Like a super deluxe edition of "Extreme Home Makeover" no job was too big or difficult. Jesus taught that in spite of all our junk, mistakes, and errors...we are still "love worthy" to the Father.

Love bears up under anything and everything that comes, is ever ready to believe the best of every person, its hopes are fadeless under all circumstances and it endures everything (without weakening). Love never fails – never fades out or becomes obsolete or comes to an end.

– I Corinthians 13: 7–8a, *Amplified Bible*[36]

THE POWER OF BLESSING
ON THE ROAD WITH YESHUA – NOTES FROM DISCIPLE #7

It's been a long and hot day at the end of a long, hard week. There are thousands of people milling around after the Rabbi's teaching. Many of the town leaders and teachers from Jerusalem wait for a one-on-one word with Rabbi Yeshua. You and the other disciples are in charge of crowd control and trying to figure out who's next in line

---

[36] *The Amplified New Testament, The Four Translations New Testament.*

to talk with Him. The Rabbi looks tired; you are definitely tired and can't wait to eat. Then while your back is turned, all these children dart through the crowd. In an instant a dozen of them are wrapped around his legs, climbing into his lap and hanging off of his arms. Their mothers trail behind carrying infants, who push through wanting the Rabbi to lay hands and speak words of blessing over their babies.

Naturally, to you this looks like things are out of control. This is no time for kissing the babies and taking photos. There are important adults waiting for a moment of Yeshua's time. So with a glance to the other talmid (disciples) you start to shoo the children off and push the mothers to the back of the line. Oops, big mistake!

People were bringing little children to Jesus to have him touch them, but the disciples rebuked them. When Jesus saw this, he was indignant. He said to them, "Let the little children come to me, and do not hinder them, for the kingdom of God belongs to such as these. I tell you the truth, anyone who will not receive the kingdom of God like a little child will never enter it." And he took the children in his arms, put his hands on them and blessed them.

– Mark 10: 13–16, *NIV*

Jesus loved children and was never too busy to speak, embrace or bless them. There is a Power of Blessing that we have forgotten in our world. In a world filled with curses and millions of words it is hard to believe that being blessed would have any

back the mortgage paid on your death sentence. You got a first class ticket to the main dining room. Welcome to the unbelievable existence in which miracles are ordinary and the eternal more tangible than your lunch.

Jesus unlocked the prison doors of birth, gender, culture, family, and society. He offered citizenship in the Kingdom. He gave people the right to be sons of God instead of slaves to a system. As one saint said, "I am not a physical being having a spiritual experience, I am a spiritual being having a temporal–physical experience."

Don't Forget
the Children!

Children are the hope and future of our world. It has been said that we have a "Fatherless Generation" but I believe that we have a "Parentless Generation" of children. With divorce rates, working moms, economic hardships, disease, addictions, the children pay the highest ticket price. You don't have to take a trip overseas, just walk around the corner to a daycare center. There are dozens of children who would love to be held and loved. Or see if a single mom or young couple would like an afternoon off while you take the kids. If you have the time and room in your heart there are many children needing homes and a stable environment.

One couple I know adopted a group of three siblings from the Ukraine, which added to their own children making six.

One of my passions is helping orphans around the world. The world now has the largest population of orphans ever known. There are many fine organizations that are working hard to help, but so much more is needed. Simply providing food for an orphan or nutrition for an orphanage makes a difference.

power. In scripture the impact of curses last three to four generations but the impact of blessings last for a 1,000 generations or 20,000 years. It is hard to comprehend the magnitude of that promise. Personally, I would be happy with a small bucket beside the computer desk that automatically refills when I need a splash or two.

In the Jewish tradition of the Friday evening Shabbat there is a time of blessing in which the father looks his family members in the eyes and blesses them. What a wonderful opportunity to lovingly affirm and bless your children. If you were a disciple of Jesus' then that meant that Friday night would have been unforgettable. Imagine what it must have been like to have Jesus look you in the eyes and speak blessings and life-giving words into your spirit.

APPLICATION

It is important to speak words of encouragement and blessing. Life is difficult for us all, so why not use the power of your words for positive means. As we discussed in earlier chapters there is a difference between the spirit, soul and body. Speaking blessings is more than saying "bless you" when someone sneezes. When we speak blessings we affirm the character, integrity, giftings, love, service, talents, insights and dedication that we see in another person. For some great resources that discuss how to develop and bless the Human Spirit, I recommend Arthur Burk's materials.[37]

---

[37] Arthur Burk, Plumbline Ministries.

THE POWER OF JOY AND HUMOR

If you have no joy in your religion, there's a leak in your Christianity somewhere.
– W.A. ("Billy") Sunday

Did Jesus use Humor? I hope so, in fact I am confident of it for several reasons. First, how many crowds do you know that will forgo food, sleep and comfort for a depressing Shakespearean monologue? Not many that I know of, unless of course it is a select crowd with a high tendency toward manic-depression. People don't stand in the hot sun with crying babies unless the teacher is dynamic, and puts on a good "show." Laughter is the fastest way to connect to an audience, and Jesus did that very well.

As far as "dramatic value and suspense," Jesus delivered. In a world with oral tradition, Jesus was the best show in town. In the "debate and wit" category, he won every encounter with high scores. They were amazed with his "curve ball" questions that baffled the "know-it-alls" and people couldn't wait to hear what Jesus would say next.

Did Jesus laugh? Yes. Did he take joy in his disciples and the people he healed, absolutely! He rejoiced when the disciples returned from their first solo ministry trips. He celebrated and found joy in fulfilling his purpose. Joy and laughter help strengthen us so that we accomplish our work. Like rain to a dry and weary land, so is laughter among friends.

Never lend you car to anyone to whom you have given birth.
– Erma Bombeck

JOY FOR LIFE!

Joy is critical to a child's well-being and future success. When a child feels the joy of their parents it builds their confidence and internal security. A child needs to feel the joy of laughing, creating, hugging, resting, playing, sharing, just being held in the arms of loving adults. The happy experiences help fill up the "joy reservoir" that a child draws upon when life is difficult. For example the child falls while running and after crying for a few seconds starts to laugh when the dad does something funny. The amount of joy that a child is accustomed to affects their ability as an adult to respond to change and stress. That means that the greater the ability to laugh, the easier it is to overcome difficulties, and to respond positively to change and life's challenges.

Laughter and joy is also healthy. Research shows that laughter and positive attitudes contribute to stronger immune systems and contribute to faster healing.

Laughter is also good for business. In my training sessions, we find that joy and laughter is essential and refreshing. Laughter improves performance, creativity and problem solving. Laughter helps to "recharge the brain" because it stimulates both sides of the brain. Joy reduces stress and interpersonal conflict. Laughter and joy are like a huge positive magic wand that helps to neutralize the bad stuff that gums up relationships and our brains.

One of my clients manages a software development team for a finance organization. She makes everyone pause around 4 p.m. for a "Hoola Hoop Break." This fun refresher gets everyone away from the computer and gives him or her the energy to finish the day's tasks.

APPLICATION

Positive energy is life-giving and it reproduces itself. The same is true with a great joke, funny story, miracle, or remarkable event. People retell the story and laugh. Today find ways to share a laugh with two new people. Find creative ways to increase the joy level in the office or at home to build the fun and recharge the batteries.

MODELING LOVE

You learn to speak by speaking, to study by studying, to run by running, to work by working; and just so you learn to love God and man by loving. Begin as a mere apprentice and the very power of love will lead you on to become a master of the art. – St. Francis D. Sales

In the previous chapter we saw how Jesus helped to prepare his followers with simple rituals that had meaning and would build their spiritual lives. The disciples were taught to remember him by eating the bread and the wine. But on his final night with them, Jesus did something very unusual. John writes, *"having loved His own who were in the world, He loved them to the end." –* John 13: 1b, *HCBC.*

As the evening meal was served, Jesus did something very unusual for a rabbi. He removed his outer clothing, wrapped a towel around his waist, poured water in a basin and washed his disciples' feet. Jesus performed a task that was usually left to the lowest of slaves or the youngest children. Jesus shocked the disciples, so much so that Peter first refused (out of honor to the rabbi).

After washing their feet, He said that he had done this so they might do the same for each other. In this simple act of bathing, Jesus established a foundational principle of his life and philosophy. The principle of servant leader has never been more clearly demonstrated than in this one simple act. When you see that something is dirty, don't complain – just get the towel out.

There is a new leadership model for corporate and business leaders, which is the "Servant Leader Model." This is a common term and goal for those individuals, corporations and groups who care for their communities. Hurricane Katrina, 9/11 and other disasters have demonstrated the remarkable sacrifice and commitment of the wonderful American people. One reason the United States has been blessed is because of the unprecedented amount of foreign aid we pour into other people's lives.

Summary

Just as a gardener delights in the beauty of the flowers, when we communicate in love we will see the hearts and spirits of others come alive. When we learn to pour the water of love into the parched hearts of others, we will see eyes brighten, faces smile, hear voices singing and watch transformations more incredible than any butterfly to ever have flown. Love is the ingredient that can heal the hearts, awake the sleeping and make the flame leap with joy. Life is in the power of the tongue, but the transformation begins with words of love.

Jesus represents the greatest Servant Leader Model the world has ever known. He connected and reconnected people through love that was honest and pure. His love was a mirror so people could see the truth within their own hearts. Jesus' love set a new bar for how we should treat each other. His love was a bridge that connected people to themselves, each other and God. He allows us to touch and be touched through his love.

When we take time to focus on the needs and concerns of others, it empowers us to be more loving. Selfishness is one of the first prisons that a person must conquer. The second is the throne of pride. When we learn to live, walk and talk in love, we discover a joy beyond expectations. Love is passion's highest goal and passion is love's highest expression. For Jesus, his passion fueled his love and love carried his passion.

CHAPTER 9
EXECUTION – PRECISION AND ACTION

Accomplishing any goal requires consistent focus. Execution is the final technique of the S.I.M.P.L.E.™ Method. Execution is critical. It requires energy, precision, commitment and accurate focus. Jesus reached his goals because he executed and hit the target whenever he communicated. His examples were clear, his questions concise, and his responses precise. He never let others pull him off track with their personal agendas and schedules.

Imagine hitting the target or making the score every time you tried. How exciting! How do we respond when our favorite players complete the pass, make the birdie putt, or smash the grand slam homerun out of the park? Athletes must have skill and precision.

Now think of a surgeon. Imagine the focus and precision it takes to clear a clogged artery or to remove a blood clot from the brain. How much concentration and skill does that take? What sort of doctor do you want when you have major surgery? Do you want someone who is thorough and complete in what they do?

How do you measure precision?

Batting 400 means the player is successful 40% of the time. Now, would you want a surgeon with a 40% success rate? For a doctor, we want a 100% success rate. Both of these scenarios require focus and precision, but they measure success differently.

When people consider their communication technique, they often have the wrong glasses on. They approach their communication opportunities with a sports-eye, hit and miss approach, instead of using the laser focus of a surgeon's eye.

To become a Master Communicator requires more than luck, it requires discipline and skill working together. They are willing to make the personal sacrifice to achieve the goal. They have the discipline and will power to prepare and rehearse. Focus unifies the message. Precision increases strength. Execution drives the message toward the target like a missile.

Empowered communicators take control and ensure that the full cycle of communication is accomplished. They are aware of the message content, how it connects to the audience, is transmitted and is received by the listeners. Proper execution maximizes the impact and helps create response from the listener. Execution is the fuel that helps complete the communication cycle.

Execution is the final and most critical communication technique that Jesus used. Let's revisit the parable of "the Sower and the seed" and Jesus' response to it. Jesus did not waste his energy on people who were hard headed. He cared about the seed he planted. He looked for fruit that would remain.

In order to be focused and an empowered communicator, it is important to understand the way in which Jesus operated during everyday situations and conflicts. Here are some characteristics that we notice about his performance:

- Always on target with his stories, questions, and responses.
- Never let others sabotage his mission.
- The expectations and agendas of others did not pull him off course (including family, friends, leaders and adversaries).
- Never distracted by rejection, accusations, or criminal proceedings.
- He refused to be defined by terms and rules of social religiosity.
- Jesus knew who he was, why he was here and what he had to do.

WHAT'S THE REAL QUESTION?

The ability to execute requires a deep and thorough understanding of purpose. Purpose requires that one has mastered the questions – Who am I? Why am I here? What is my purpose?

Like stars in the sky, these questions have shaped the galaxies of civilizations. These questions are the bedrock of great literature, movies and songs. In the musical *A Chorus Line*, one actor sings a prayer:

Who am I anyway? Am I my resume that is a picture of a person I don't know?
What does he want from me? What should I try to be?
So many faces all around and here we go.
I need this job, oh God, I need this show![38]

This song echoes the feelings that every heart utters. We are on a quest for pieces of the puzzle with our name on them. Sometimes we are graced with a glimpse of how our pieces fit into life's constellations. But most of us are perplexed. We simply enjoy watching the stars dance across the heavens.

Jesus was able to execute because like a good business plan or public relations campaign, he had answered three key questions:

WHO AM I? OR WHO'S YOUR DADDY?

There's a great deal of confidence that comes from knowing that your dad is the boss. Jesus heard, "This is my son, in whom I am well pleased." He had daily conversations with Dad. "My Father, who art in heaven." When he was challenged, he pointed to the source of his authority – "My Father and I are one."

WHY AM I HERE?

Jesus understood his mission and he communicated what it was through many techniques including analogies and direct statements. He knew it was to do the will of His Father and not to stop until the new contract was fully executed.

[38] *I Hope I Get It*, A Chorus Line Music: Marvin Hamlisch; Lyrics: Edward Kleban; Book: Nicholas Dante & James Kirkwood. Premiere: Tuesday, April 15, 1975.

HOW DO I ACCOMPLISH THE MISSION?

People are the best assets of any company. Jesus knew that his sheep would carry his message to the world. He prepared for opposition and evil. He encountered both.

The Lord gave you two ends – one for sitting and one for thinking. Your success depends on which one you use – heads you win, tails you lose.
– Gas Flame

THE IMPORTANCE OF TRUE NORTH

Before there were compasses, ancient maps had a very different orientation. Maps used the East or the sun to form the vertical axis. The maps were lined up so that instead of true north, true east or the light of the sun formed the direction.[39]

Often in life people ask, *"What is your true north?"* Are you headed in the right direction, do you have the right map, is your compass functioning properly? When we make mistakes, many times we find that our internal compass is focused in the wrong direction. We are looking at the past, problems, or pain instead of the opportunities and abundant blessings that surround us.

In the famous movie, *White Christmas*, Bing Crosby crooned the words, *"When I am worried and I can't sleep, I count my blessings instead of sheep. And I go to sleep counting my blessings."* What a great practice. It is critical to remind ourselves and others year round that a grateful attitude makes the spirit grow. Arthur Burk teaches, "I pray that you are blessed with the ability to glance at your problems and gaze at your Father."[40]

It is said that what we gaze upon we become like. Jesus had the amazing ability to focus beyond circumstances. Regardless of where the road went, Jesus never lost his way because he knew what his true north was. Even when others tried to pull him off track he kept all parts of his internal compass (spiritual, emotional, mental and physical) set in the right direction.

---

[39] John Noble Wilford, *The Mapmakers, The story of the Great Pioneers in Cartography from Antiquity to Space Age*, org Alfred A. Knopf, Inc., New York, NY, 1981.
[40] Burke, Arthur, Plumbline Ministries, ref. earlier.

I am the light of the world. Anyone who follows me will never walk in darkness but will have the light of life. – John 8: 12

SIMPLE COMMUNICATION SAVES LIVES ... AND TIME!

On a practical business level, remember the "KISS" principle? I first heard this principle from my dad, who had this drummed into him while a young cadet at West Point. In case you don't know – KISS stands for Keep It Simple, Solider. Now other folks use other "s words," depending on cultural choices, but solider works for our purposes.

Master Communicators enhance their messages with clear, easily understood words and phrases. They avoid jargon, except when they customize examples for a special group or situation.

APPLICATION

Keep communication simple. Use headlines and summary points, especially for updates and emails. Take the time to condense and compress before presentations. The best chefs learn to reduce their broths to concentrates which increases flavor. Take the hint. Reduce your messages to give them more strength and to make them more palatable to the audience.

Remember the business plan discipline that requires a one sentence, one paragraph and one page summary before the detailed report? For emails, use the header to the max. Instead of simply responding with "re:re:re:" use the subject line to answer and advance the information flow. Which would you read first – "Re:re Project" or "On track – Quick Question"?

MIND READING – IS IT POSSIBLE?

Have you ever had a person who could answer your unspoken questions as if they were reading your thoughts? How does that feel? Even though it is fun to watch Councilor Troy, on Star Trek read the thoughts of the other humanoids, that's a sci-fi fantasy. It is a bit unsettling to have someone address a hidden issue. We often feel conflicted. One part wants the answer, while the other part wants the person to shut up so that others don't learn our thoughts. Truth is not always comfortable. When truth is ugly, people may choose to hide it.

Time after time, question after question, Jesus hit the bull's eye. He was able to execute responses that were exactly what a person needed to hear. It may not have been what the person wanted to hear.

When he spoke with the Samaritan woman at the well, he answered her need.[41] This famous midday conversation was unusual for three reasons – the person, their gender and the time. In Jesus' time Jews usually didn't interact with the Samaritans and it was highly unusual for a man to be talking to an unknown woman who was a social outcast. Trips to the water well were like the early morning meeting around the coffee pot. This woman came to the well in the heat of the day because she wanted to avoid people. Her colorful past with five husbands had probably been the source of much rejection and abuse. When Jesus asked her for a drink she was suspicious and pushed back with questions. Yet, her honesty allowed him to freely declare and share his purpose.

We don't know the woman's name, even though Jesus and his disciples ended up staying in the village for three productive days. First there was some verbal volleyball. "Who are you stranger?" "The well is deep." "Living water is the best." "Can I have a drink, please?"

Jesus told her to go get her husband. She said, "I don't have a husband." He told her that didn't matter – but go get the man she was living with, so that he could talk to them both. Naturally she was stunned, as anyone would be. "Who has he been talking to? How much does he know?"

So in a perfectly normal blocking action – the woman changed the course of the conversation by asking a theological question. "Enough about me; let's talk religion."

---

[41] John 4: 7–26, The Samaritans were considered lower class to other Jews. They had intermarried when the Assyrians had settled the northern Kingdom. Travelers walking from Galilee to southern Judea would lengthen their trip by walking around Samaritan territory. Jesus had just come from the Jordan where he had been baptizing. The Pharasees were trying to stir up trouble between he and John by comparing the numbers baptized (see the section on Borg Game's – Let's Play Competition). When the disciples returned from finding some food, they were shocked to find Jesus talking with a Samaritan female, of questionable reputation.

Jesus sidestepped and got back on track. He said that the day was coming when true faith would be expressed with genuine devotion rather than meaningless repetitive acts.

The woman's heart of faith leapt. "Yes, the anointed one is coming, I know it!"

Then Jesus said, "He's looking at you, kid!" She was thrilled and became his first publicist.

DEALING WITH ROCKY ROADS

Even though we may know who we are and have a clearly focused mission, the journey is never easy or smooth. Life has a lot of mountains, potholes and detours that have to be traversed. Sometimes the road has roadblocks, pitfalls and swamps created by others. Human roadblocks are often more challenging because they come from negative emotions such as pride, envy, jealousy, gossip, resentment, control, bitterness, slander and many more.

These obstacles come from humans but are they really human or un-human? "Inhumane" is a term describing actions, which are cruel, barbarous, savage of heart and unfeeling. I would like to propose using the term "un-human" to describe actions and emotions that destroy community. Even though it is impossible to ignore the evil that lurks in the hearts of men, I believe that at their best mankind is loving, creative and productive.[42] Jesus was prepared to encounter resistance and opposition that was un-human and inhumane.

RESISTANCE IS NORMAL, NOT FUTILE!

Borg has become a popular term to describe an oppressive organization, working conditions or individuals who are manipulative and controlling regardless of moral issues. The term "Borg" originated from the Star Trek television series. The Borg were a fictional race of cyborgs – humaniods who are part cybernetic machines. They were considered the greatest threat of the Galaxies.

---

[42] The definition of what is man at their best is important. A person at their best is when they have a personal relationship with God and have a level of maturity (spiritual, personal and physical) that serves others and the world with a heart of generosity and love.

They were like locusts, consuming planets and their resources. They traveled in square space ships. The individuals they captured were made into drones or slave zombies that were connected to the hive mind with implants and probes. An individual's identity and will were suppressed by the Borg mind. People served the hive as "one of nine." The famous Borg saying which has become a cultural icon is, "Resistance is futile." But the Borg was wrong. Our favorite Star Trek heroes always save the day. For the Federation, resistance is always successful when fighting evil aliens.

BEWARE OF THE EYES OF BORG

Borgs. We all have had bad jobs and social situations, which seemed laden with Borgs even if we didn't know what to call them. Jesus encountered many groups, Pharisees, Sadducees, Scribes, Heriodians, High Priests and Romans who represented the religious, financial, educational, and political interests of his time.

Many from these categories of people were righteous and noteworthy. Others were not. Those who were not came against him. Time and history tells us that within every organization there are those who seek control for their own purposes. The struggles in Jerusalem in Jesus' time were no different than we see today.

To help describe the un-human actions and evil forces that resisted Jesus' destiny and that resist our own destinies, I will use the term Borg. Feel free to substitute your own terms; some of my other favorite terms are turkeys, little brains, critters or character builders. Sometimes those you love and work with may start acting like a Borg or put on a turkey suit. In that case, don't take it personally, but wait 'til the phase passes. My grandfather, Pop-pop, used to say, "Honey, you just have to love 'em the way they are."

Identifying our enemy is important. Who fights and resists us? What are they planning? This helps us form strategies. It builds our inner resilience. Jesus was able to communicate exactly the way he intended because he knew his purpose. He saw the goal beyond his adversaries. He did not let the comparisons and questions cause him to miss a step.

Even Jesus had to deal with evil aliens and Borg-like people throughout his life. As discussed in the Preparation chapter, Jesus encountered the major bad dude at the end of his forty-day fast. (At least it was an easy camping trip to pack for.) Fasting helps strengthen the spirit and makes it easy to deal with challenges, temptations and evil aliens like Lucifer.

BEWARE ASSIMILATION!

Have you every heard someone say, "You're so different. You are so unique; you're so special"? Now sometimes they mean it. Other times they may mean that you are weird. "Why don't you act like us?"

Jesus dealt with a truckload of comments that were laden with subtle messages – and some not so subtle. He heard comments such as these:

You don't talk like us.

You don't teach like us.

You don't walk like us.

You don't pray like us.

You don't follow laws the way we follow them.

You don't wash like us.

You don't eat like us.

You don't preach like us.

You don't care about your reputation like we care about ours.

And you go around healing people on the Sabbath.

In fact you are nothing like us at all.

How is it that you can heal people?

The Great Resistor

If you were to give a job description to the ultimate evil alien or the devil, what would it be? After the trite list of his actions: hatred, jealousy, envy, lying, stealing, natural disasters, wars, famine, plagues, curses, diseases, headaches, murders, genocide, pornography, you might list some of his titles.

Not to glorify Satan, but he has many names and descriptions worth a few moments' consideration. The devil or Satan has many names in both the Old and New Testaments, including: accuser of brethren, angel of light, prince of the power of the air, the liar, the deceiver, the father of lies, and Lucifer. Satan means "adversary" in Hebrew and the Greek name, "diabolos" (devil), means "one who slanders or accuses." In reviewing meaning of these names, one of the root definitions is resistance or opposer. This is why the devil is an adversary and an enemy. The first on the list of job descriptions for the devil is, "the resistor." Resistor is used more than any other term in the Bible to describe the evil one. It means that the devil gets major job security – resisting or coming against all that which is good.

How can you cast demons out of the lunatics?
How'd you do that?
Why is it that when you pray for the crazy-heads, they get better?
Where do you plug into that power anyway?
Say, who are you, anyway?

I wonder what the everyday village rabbis thought about Jesus. How did they process what happened around him? What did the establishment people think? With all the strange happenings, or miracles, I wonder if they thought Jesus was from another world?

APPLICATION

Don't be swayed by the criticisms of others. Those that swim against the stream do make waves. Remember that the Borg are everywhere! It is important to stay focused and deliver your message. Don't let the rejection of the Borg affect your passion to communicate what's on your mind. Don't let a Borg's opinion affect you. Put the criticisms of the Borgs and the turkeys into the proper context – stuff them.

Become so wrapped up in something that you forget to be afraid.
– Lady Bird Johnson

DEALING WITH THE BORGS

STEP ONE – MEETING THE BORG EXPECTATIONS

One of the hardest challenges of growing up is dealing with the expectations of our family, especially our parents. Before she died, an elderly friend of mine grieved that she hadn't let her son pursue the athletic career that he loved. Instead he was pushed into a business career that lead to destructive behavior patterns that took him years to resolve. Family relationships can be empowering or restricting.

Some families have hand-me-downs that look like lovely designer clothes but are really nets of control. When we look closely we can read the labels – guilt, shame, duty, inner vows, rejections, scapegoat, family honor and other wearer beware instructions. These nets of expectations are invisible but they are stronger and more restrictive than any net of steel.

We all hope our families are a sanctuary where we can feel safe. It is true that there is no place like home. Our souls need a safe place to live, love, rest, and grow. One of the best pieces of advice on marriage that I ever heard was, "Make sure that you give each other permission and enough space to grow into the people you were meant to be." That attitude is a true sign of mature love. Jesus and his mother Mary demonstrated that their love was rich and mature.

WHAT ABOUT THE WINE?

I wonder if at the wedding feast, Mary thought about basic logistics when she pointed out to Jesus that they ran out of wine? As a mom in a tight knit community, she had to be sensitive to the fact that her grown son had brought a whole pack of unexpected guests (disciple-wanna-be's) to the wedding. Running out of wine would have been a huge embarrassment to the hosts. Mary knew that if she went to her son, he could solve the problem. Maybe Jesus could collect a coin or two from this unusual assortment of men, who followed him. Mary wasn't expecting a miracle, as a mom she knew that Jesus needed to help solve the problem that his new career launch had perpetrated.

Switching gears a moment, let's think about working out at the gym and how the term resistance is used. Personal trainers can give you a lecture about how important resistance and stretching is to muscle tone. Not that we fully appreciate and enjoy the pain, but we do love it when the muscles look good.

So resistance makes our muscles stronger and more attractive. Does the same thing apply for our character and spiritual muscles? Maybe all those people who step on our nerves – the Borgs – are simply there to help us build more muscles. Maybe next time, instead of getting depressed when there is resistance, we need to just give it the ultimate pushback and finish the reps. Who knew there exists a positive side for dealing with Borgs? Would we be who we are if we had never faced resistance?

When we meet with resistance to plans and goals, allow it to become an opportunity to build the muscles of discipline and inner strength. Or, kick it up a notch and turn your soul into a resistor of resistance. Allow that to energize you to the next level. Resistance comes with the territory when pushing forward to meet a goal.

I love how Mary dealt with this issue. When Jesus said, "My time has not yet come," she said nothing. Her response was wonderful. No word of rebuttal, no argument, and no explanation. She simply turned and told the servants to do whatever Jesus requested. The woman knew her son. The servants followed her instructions, which shows that Mary was probably helping with the wedding celebration.

Mary presented the problem. She challenged Jesus for a solution, provided assistance and then let go in faith. Jesus responded with a very curious order. He said to fill the jugs with water. I would love to know what went through Mary's head as she watched the servants fill the huge jars with over 120 gallons of water. That is more water than four bathtubs; at four gallons a pop it represents more than thirty trips to the well. Depending on the number of servants helping, Operation Water Jugs would have taken two to four hours real time.

Do you think Mary wondered what Jesus was going to do with all that water? Was he going to use it for washing? Was he going to do some sort of baptism like John? Mary was accustomed to Jesus doing the unusual. From the first words of the angel Gabriel she had learned to wait and watch. Within a few hours, Mary learned the answer. Jesus' action declared his purpose. The water of baptism became the wine of a new covenant.

Jesus respected his mother's request even if it wasn't the right time. He was genuine.

Mary challenged Jesus to step into his destiny. She presented the need, without guilt or personal expectation, and a miracle resulted. It wasn't on the schedule, but what's a good son to do? Was it God's perfect timing for a miracle? Who knows?

One thing for certain, his mother was surprised when it happened. Who knew?

PRESSURES FROM THE BROTHERS AND THE HOMEBOYS

Now, dealing with good old mom is one thing, but how do you handle the brothers and the homeboys? The brothers and homeboys cover your back and are the muscle that makes things happen. Conventional wisdom knows that making big things happen requires teamwork and relationships, lots of relationships. If you get crosswise with your team, it can be disastrous. King Arthur had his knights. Luke Skywalker had the Jedi and even the short dude with big feet, Frodo had the Fellowship of the Ring frat brothers. It can be hard when the heat from the team is on!

Jesus had to deal with his brothers and their personal agendas throughout his ministry. At the beginning of his ministry he was teaching and his family showed up on location. Someone told Jesus they were waiting to see him. At first this seems like a simple family visit to the popular new teacher. But it really was more than that to the group. This was at the beginning of Jesus' ministry. Rumors about who he was and what he was doing flew all over the place. As with any new charismatic leader, there are many who wanted to take advantage of the opportunity to advance.

Jesus used the analogy of family to communicate what his purpose was to the crowd. He used the interactive question *"Who are my mother and brothers?"* Then he answered by gesturing to the crowd encircling him. He used a figurative analogy. *"Here are my mother and my brothers! Whoever does the will of God is my brother and sister and mother."* – Mark 3: 34–35, *HSCB*.

It was a brilliant response. Rather than directly confronting them and telling them that they had it wrong, yet again, he used the interactive question followed by an analogy to shut down their expectations. He redirected their focus back to the spiritual work he was doing.

The crowd wanted to see how Jesus related to his family's expectations that the family/tribe would be honored and elevated. In Middle-Eastern culture the tribe and all the family members, brothers, cousins, relatives all benefit when the king or leader comes from their bloodlines. The crowds and the leaders watched and listened to see if Jesus was building a power base with his family. A power base could be used for political and social gain. As a strategy,

Jesus could gain a power base of men, combine it with popularity and develop an army to rise up against the Romans. Would he do that?

Jesus didn't let their expectations for political success change his direction. Instead he immediately reaffirmed his purpose and the scope of his mission. He explained that those who do God's will are his family. He reframed their questions. He explained that his agenda was heavenly, rather than political.

APPLICATION

Clearly communicate your purpose and stay focused. Do not let the expectations of others pull you off track. If others try to hook us into their agendas, it is important to clarify your purpose to them immediately. If they try to corner you in public, then use analogies to avoid direct conflict with others who misunderstand. When you respond to the expectations of the crowd and the needs that you have not identified as your concern or responsibility, it changes your direction. Keep the purpose and passion of your destiny as the true compass for your life.

MORE FUN WITH BORGS – TA-TA-T-TIMING!

One of the more devious tricks of the Borgs is to mess up a person's timing. If you can't be stopped, then it is a common warfare strategy to call an army to war before they are ready for battle. Even though you may have the potential to win an Olympic medal, if you arrive for competition before you are ready, the result could be devastating. Recognize that sometimes people you love and who may have the best intentions, may try to push you into something before the time is right – before you are ready. Check your watch, your calendar and your GPS.

Jesus had ministered for several years. It was time for the Feast of Tabernacles. Some of Jesus' brothers wanted him to come to the feast and teach in the temple. With the crowds four to five times their normal size, they saw it as a great opportunity to help Jesus hit the big time. It was a terrific idea and Jesus' brothers and disciples were all ready to be the advance team, set up the meetings, pay for the lunches, everything. Great idea, but wrong timing. Jesus refused to go with them. Half way through the festival, when everyone had been talking about him, Jesus showed up and started teaching. Talk about great timing. As expected the religious leaders were amazed as to how someone, without a pedigreed background of degrees, family or training, could communicate with such power.

APPLICATION

Remember great timing is the secret for effective execution. Be honest about when you are ready to take the next big step. Don't let others move you out of position.

BEGINNING BORG GAMES – LET'S PLAY COMPETITION

Some major destructive tactics of Borgs are to start rumors, set up opposition, and send in competition. It is easy to see this happening in politics, business, court cases and even in religion and in churches. Sometimes businesses even play dirty and plant a false story to discredit the competition. On a personal level, most of us have dealt with the rejection and cruelty that can come from our peers at some time.

Popularity always stirs up envy and jealousy. Bob Sorge's book, *Envy: The Enemy Within*[43] is an excellent and convicting source on this interpersonal poison. Envy is a very subtle and dangerous emotion because it likes to twist itself around gossip, slander and murder. Envy sparks the fire, gossip fans the flame and bitterness keeps the coals red-hot.

Jesus didn't have to wait for people to become jealous. In the first months of his ministry, after he helped out with wine at the wedding, Jesus and his disciples went down to the Judean countryside. John the Baptist likely hung out here because there was lots of water around for baptizing.

Things went well. Huge crowds came from all over to hear the preaching and to be baptized. Things were fine until someone got into a fight with one of John's disciples. They complained that Jesus had bigger crowds than they did. John told his guys to chill because Jesus was the real deal.

---

[43] Envy: The Enemy Within by Bob Sorge, Copyright 2003 Gospel Light/Regal Books, Ventura, CA , for more information on Bob Sorge go to www.oasishouse.net.

When crisis or painful and perplexing events happen it is easy to ask, "Why?" This is not always productive. Bill Johnson relates, "Instead of asking God, Why? I have learned to instead ask two questions, 'What are you doing, Father?' and 'What is the next thing that I am to do?' This helps to keep my eye on the mark and pushing toward the goal. I may not understand what is going on, but I do trust His love and stayed pointed in the right direction."[44]

Later, when Pharisees couldn't draw a crowd, they grew jealous, and started keeping score. Rather than celebrating the great number of people trying to clean up their lives, the Pharisees turned into play-by-play announcers at a swim meet. They started to tell everyone that Jesus' disciples were baptizing more people than John baptized. Jesus learned they turned it into a competition at John's expense. They were slamming John. Jesus took action. To everyone's surprise, he shut things down and headed for the hills.

John had prepared the way for him. Jesus honored him. Jesus could have stayed at the Jordan where there were good crowds, good offerings and great exposure. But when the integrity of John's ministry was threatened by malicious gossip, Jesus responded with integrity and pulled up stakes. He refused to let the competitive games of the Borg destroy John.

DOING THE STUFF! ACTIONS COUNT

"Wisdom is proved right by her actions."
– Jesus, Matthew 11: 19b, *NIV*

So much of our experiences and thoughts are lived in the virtual and fantasy realities of television, films, internet and video games that it is hard to remember that experience is the best teacher. The basic rule says, "Words are nice, but only trust actions." Expressions like "Show me the Money!" or "Where's the Beef?" reflect the desire to see

---

[44] Bill Johnson, The Amber Rose Conference, March 1–3, 2007, Shady Grove Church, Grand Praire, TX. Bill Johnson is an author and Senior Pastor of Bethel Church in Redding, CA.

the proof. Jesus said, "A tree is known by its fruit," and "Wisdom is proved right by its actions."

When things are rough and we feel trapped, it is easy to doubt. John the Baptist got terrific response by the Jordan. He knew that Jesus was the man. Thrown into prison by Herod, he sent a discouraged message to Jesus. "Are you the one?"

John had to talk in code because to say the M-word meant an immediate death penalty. But John asked Jesus, "Hey Cuz, if you're the Messiah sent to end oppression, then when are you coming to get me out of this jail cell? Did you know Herod's wife figures on wasting me?"

Jesus' response was based on the six signs of the Messiah found in Isaiah. *"Report to John what you hear and see: the blind see, the lame walk, those with skin disease are healed, the deaf hear, the dead are raised, and the poor are told the good news. And if anyone is not offended because of me, he is blessed."* – Matthew 11: 2–6, HCBC.

Rather than hype, Jesus pointed out his actions. He was doing the stuff – the right stuff! Jesus demonstrated his purpose and authority by pointing to his deeds. The miracles are here. What other the proof do you need? Jesus did something similar when questioned by his adversaries. He pointed to his deeds and asked what fault they found with them.

When John asked Jesus if he could expect a rescue, he didn't get the answer he wanted to hear. Jesus' answer was also in code but it avoids the mention of "setting captives free." Excluding this phrase seems to indicate that Jesus may have been diplomatically saying that even though he is the Anointed one, he doesn't have the "get out of jail free" card.[45] Jesus communicated, don't be upset if I don't do what you want me to do. Remember God is executing a very big plan. You've done great with your part.

APPLICATION

Let your actions demonstrate your purpose and authority. When people wanted proof, Jesus pointed to his track record. Your

---

[45] Page 42. Stern, David H., the *Jewish New Testament Commentary*, Jewish New Testament Publications, Inc. 1992, Clarksville, MD.

works should be an extension of the authority and purpose of your destiny and call.

SUMMARY

Jesus communicated with the precision of a laser. His personal discipline, preparation and will helped him succeed in any situation. As a communicator, he was able to answer people's questions, even when they didn't voice them. He was not distracted from his mission by family members, followers, the Borg or any of the games people play. His focus was impeccable. When Jesus communicated, he expected response.

When he spoke to a broken body, it healed. When he spoke to the storm, it stopped. When he spoke to demons, they left. When Jesus spoke to his pupils, they learned. His words had authority. Even the temple guards, when asked why they didn't arrest him, said that they had never heard anyone speak with the amount of authority that Jesus had. His words compelled his followers to respond. The seeds that Jesus planted were about a new Kingdom and a new reality. When people asked for proof of this Kingdom, he told them that the blind see, the lame walk, the lepers are healed, the dead live, the deaf hear and the prisoners are set free.

PROFILE
PONTIUS PILATE – THE JESUS FILES

He looks upon the faces of the ugly mob as they yell, "Crucify him." It makes no sense. There is no reason, no logic, and no way out. Think. Think once more, what can be done? Is there a way to escape this labyrinth of deception? How did this happen?

What of this man Yeshua? What had he done to make the mob so mad? They were insane with rage. Never had he seen them buzzing like wasps together at the same task. He could feel the threatening hum in his gut, but it was impossible to see inside the hive. He knew a lynch mob when he saw one. He hated it. This was even worse than the weeklong siege during his first week in Judea. They, at least, had been zealous for faith. This group was zealous with a hatred that made his skin crawl. Even the leaders, who had always cloaked their hatred, showed their venom running through the mob, prodding it like coals.

Dealing with these Jews was more difficult than he had dreamed. Such brilliant minds! Others were fanatics. Some sounded pious, others trustworthy, but they always argued and questioned everything.

These people defied logic. They ran on passion and law that in a hundred lifetimes you could never understand. This portion of the Empire was worse than the backside of the unwashed Germanic hordes. It was easier to battle the blue-skinned Gauls than to deal with the web of manipulation called Jerusalem.

This was an ambush, a cruel nightmare that seemingly would not end. Why had they bothered him so early? No decent Roman would petition before noon. It was barely dawn when they awoke the household with their incessant demands. They knew he had been up late entertaining the leading tax collectors. Before he went to bed last night, he'd reviewed the troop reports, zealot activity and riot-control plans.

Gods, how he had come to dread these festivals. It was difficult enough dealing with the crowds, the foreigners, the thieves and the zealots. Sometimes the festivals went well. Sometimes, militant factions tried to stir things up. They'd start a riot and Pilate was blamed for the killing.

Didn't Rome understand what was going on? It was a set-up for disaster. His mere 3,000 troops could only take limited action.

What an education these first three years were. No wonder no one lasted in this post. The signs should have warned him. Four predecessors came and went in twenty years. The job expectancy for Judea was not optimistic. He just hoped to survive long enough to build his reputation with Rome. It would fill the coffers and build his fortune so he could advance to a much easier position.

After all, he'd married a princess who was the granddaughter of a Caesar and the stepdaughter to the Emperor Tiberius. He'd married well and was fortunate to have found a wife who had wealth, favor at court and was loyal. Most wives preferred the luxurious baths of Rome to the deserts of Palestine. But Claudia Procula was different, she was conservative, enjoyed her children and reading. Pilate was grateful for her presence and organizational skills which made the seaside residence so pleasant.

How did he get trapped in this nightmare? This was a total ruse! The leaders were hiding something with the ridiculous accusations of this carpenter. This Yeshua was no threat. He had no weapons but words. His followers were young, uneducated, commoners and women.

He wanted to laugh and push it back like a rotten piece of meat at the market. But the intensity of the council's arguments blasted at him like the winds across the desert.

He knew better than to give the Hebrews a reason to riot. He'd tried everything to settle this matter. He'd thrown it back in their faces, stalled, and said "no," yelled, threatened, refused and tried to negotiate. For a people who loved the law, these claims made no sense. Where was the proof?

Why were they so intent on having Yeshua killed today? Even their own laws prohibited late night trials–and murder trials had to have witnesses and wait a day. They were violating their own laws. It was insanity. This man was just a clever teacher. His spies had told him about how the crowds applauded when he answered the questions and accusations of the pompous teachers in the Temple. They were just envious.

What riot had this man caused? None, except in the temple with all the greedy merchants counting money. They deserved a shakeup. He'd seen how the moneychangers cheated and inflated the prices. The priests rejected the lambs the common people brought for sacrifice, then forced them to buy those they offered.

But Yeshua? Why he wouldn't answer. Why won't he give a reason to defend him? Tell why they are wrong? Offer a shred of evidence to throw this back in the smug face of the High Priest? Yeshua's eyes – it's as if he already knows what is going to happen. How can he look so peaceful with these maniacs screaming at him? This whole trial feels like a giant pit.

"Tell me again, what has he done? Riots in Galilee and.... Where is he from again? Nazareth? Then he's a Galilean. Great, Herod can judge him. Let him deal with this mess. The man is supposed to be the King of the Jews. Why do they want to be rid of him? No matter. Get them out of my sight. We're going to have to do something."

CHAPTER 10
COMMUNICATION STRATEGIES FOR
DIFFICULT SITUATIONS

Communication is like traveling. Sometimes the trip is a thrilling adventure, other times the road is bumpy and frustrating with detours and dead-ends. A Master Communicator must be more than skillful, he or she must be an overcomer – overcoming the rough, the tough, the dirty, and the disastrous. This chapter addresses how to deal with difficult communication situations. (Now, for those of you who have skipped the rest of the book to immediately skim this chapter: Welcome, this chapter's for you. I understand the desperate feelings and stress when you need an answer in short order.)

More sleep is lost, hearts broken, money wasted, opportunities destroyed, battles fought, families shattered, spirits wounded, gifts unopened, children crushed, destruction wrought, because of poor communication. Not that poor means bad, it just means ineffective, incomplete, or undeveloped. We all have received and given poor communication. Many of our greatest regrets are the "ought nots and have-nots." ("Forgive those things we have done that we ought not to have done and those things we have not done that we ought to have done."[46]) How many situations have you replayed in your head, wishing you had not said, re-worded, or spoken up about something? Hopefully, you learned from the replay and carry the lesson with you.

All of us deal with communication difficulties, everyday. They range from the simple to the life changing. Great

---

[46] Prayer of Confession, Episcopal Book of Common Prayer.

communication means joy, love, satisfaction, laughter, weddings and babies. Bad communication causes sorrow, pain, tears, disappointment, loneliness and death. Though we may try our best to be effective and clear, we will meet all variety of resistance in life. Jesus was a magnificent communicator, yet he was horribly misunderstood. Was this his fault? No, people don't always want to hear and receive what we have to say. Sometimes the seed falls on the rocky soil and sometimes we have to keep the birds or Borg from snatching them. This chapter addresses four basic communication situations and discusses ways to deal with them. These are:

Disconnects	For one-on-one situations, personal and business.
Deceit	How to handle trick questions in public settings from those who dislike you.
Disaster	What to do in a Media Crisis when you are being manipulated or have been set up.
No-Win and Death	There are times when Jesus did not speak.

For the Disaster section, we will look at how Pontius Pilate handled the media crisis that made him famous. Believe it or not, from a media trainer's point of view, Pilate did a great job. In this classic case study, he used over a dozen different techniques to avoid disaster. I think that history has not given Pilate credit for the skill demonstrated when dealing with the Jesus crisis.

DEALING WITH DISCONNECTS

Imagine that you are working feverishly on a deadline. Your boss sticks her head in the door and asks you to meet with her in her office. As you close the door, her opening comments are, "I am concerned because there is a **communication breakdown**."

What thoughts race through your head? Do you mentally scan through emails, projects and situations? Do you start a list–What did I do? What is broken? I didn't mean to. I'm sorry. What did I miss?

How do you feel? Are you anxious, nervous, angry or shocked? What will she say next? Is this your fault and you are being corrected or fired? Or are you receiving information to help correct a problem?

What happens to your body? How does your stomach and heart rate react? Do you wish you hadn't eaten lunch? Depending on your relationship with your boss, the reactions from this could range from mild concern to gripping fear.

Now imagine the same scenario and your boss instead uses the phrase, "I am concerned because there is a **communication disconnect**."

Now what do you think, feel and respond? Do you feel as stressed or alarmed? Do you want more information? Do you think your boss is looking for solutions and suggestions? Even if the situation was caused by you, how threatened are you by a communication disconnect? If something is disconnected, you simply figure out how to reconnect. Problem solved. Move forward.

IT'S ALL IN THE TERM

The way something is said makes a huge difference. A few foolish words and you have a lawsuit. How amazing that something so small and unseen can mess things up. We all have times when the communication cycle breaks down and doesn't function. It can be at the office, home, store, in bed, classroom, courtroom or Capitol

Building. No matter where it is, we have to address the problem. There are many great books and scripts for dealing with communication situations, but in our Strategic Business Communication Training[47] we have replaced the term Communication Breakdown with Communication Disconnect.

Communication Breakdown was developed to help people talk and rebuild relationships. Unfortunately, it has been overused or used to abuse and bludgeon people instead of giving constructive criticism. As a term, Communication Breakdown has negative connotations and stirs up emotional feelings like guilt, shame, blame, fear and other similar baggage. Breakdown implies there is a personal error, fault or weakness. Breakdown makes us think that the situation is broken, in need of repair and may never be the same again.

Regardless of how successful you are, many times the term creates fear because we think that we are about to get a download of things that we have done wrong and that we need to fix. So instead of listening, people jump into a defensive foxhole and prepare for the incoming criticisms. When the scent of battle is on the wind, it is normal for people to shield themselves with explanations and load their guns with excuses.

The steps of the communication cycle are Connect, Transmit and Response. When people are afraid and defensive, it shuts down the cycle. When they hear the term "Breakdown" it is like blowing the bridge up before you can cross it. If the goal is to repair and rebuild a relationship, then why use a term like Communication Breakdown that causes more damage.

Communication Disconnect can occur at any stage in the communication cycle.

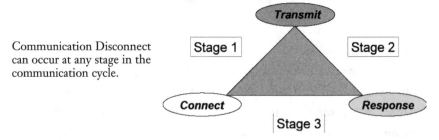

---

[47] SBCT, Strategic Business Communication Training is conducted by EmPowerCom.Us and was authored by Lynn Wilford Scarborough.

Communication disconnects can occur at any stage in the communication cycle.

USE "COMMUNICATION DISCONNECT" TO CONNECT

Communication Disconnect is a more productive term that is much easier to understand. Would you rather hear that the lamp is broken or simply unplugged? Would you rather hear that the computer is broken or just needs a battery recharge? When something is broken it can be a costly effort to repair it. When something is unplugged, we simply reach out and we are back in business.

To say we have a disconnect implies that the objective is connection (instead of guilt and blame) and that we are all working together to get communication back on line as quickly as possible. Recently, a friend and I had a scheduling conflict. As we talked it was obvious that the situation was escalating into a cycle of frustration. I pointed out to my friend that we had a communication disconnect, and rather than giving me excuses, she started listening to me. At the close of the phone call, and the following week, she told me that she really appreciated that I used the term *communication disconnect* instead of breakdown. She said that *communication breakdown* made her feel guilty and confused. Hearing the term communication disconnect made her realize that I was concerned about her needs, and was willing to reschedule our time together.

It is amazing how successful this term is in every situation, personal, business or social. We have found that this term works well when dealing with some of the tough cases. For project managers they find it reduces stress and gets the team back on track with constructive solutions.

GOT PING?

For the communication cycle there are many reasons that communication could have gone awry. When your car or computer won't run, the next step is troubleshooting. You have to figure out what is wrong. To help make an assessment we use a familiar term, "ping."

Whales, bats, submarines and airplanes use radar to navigate. They send out signals that "ping" and help them locate objects. To make sure I have a good Internet connection, I have to "ping" to see if I get bounce-back. To make sure if you have connected the rule is: **No Ping, No Thing!**

Use your senses. Look at your audience to see if they are interested or snoring. Do you have ping? Ask questions to see how people respond. Did they laugh at the joke? Are they chuckling as you describe stories? See what the response is to the tearjerker? Are they shuffling around or being still? How's it pinging for ya'?

What about that advertising or PR campaign? Is it pinging yet? Look at the reports. Are the sales numbers on track? What's traffic to the website like? Has that news story helped the stock prices? Is there Market ping?

How's the team doing? Are they pinging on all eight cylinders, or are you hearing problems with choke on the engine? Do you have pinging or knocking? Do they need a tune-up, training or hand-up? Are they joking or growling? Do they seem confused or are they building momentum? When you send out emails, how fast do they ping back with a reply?

How's the big project coming? Are things pinging along? If not, is it time to ping the customer basis with some solid research? Are you hearing the *Same Old Ping* from your top management folks? Maybe it's time to hire some experts that know how to expand your customer base with class and ping!

What did Jesus do when he had a communication disconnect? Well he used stories, questions, riddles, allegories, and confrontation to connect or reconnect. It all depended on the attitude of the person. When he discerned the reason for the disconnect, he acted accordingly. If people didn't understand the parables and information, he didn't let it bother him, but would give another example or simply move on.

APPLICATION

Next time you have a communication challenge, try using the term "communication disconnect" instead of breakdown and see if it makes things a little easier. Remember to also ask questions in the beginning to measure receptivity. Check for "ping." Watch their body language: if it says I am angry or stressed then you might want to choose another time to talk. Listen to the tone and quality of their voice.

To help evaluate the reason for a disconnect, ask, look, listen and ask more open-ended questions. Make sure that you let them finish talking before you ask another question. Ask if they have anything else they want to mention. Most problems have multiple causes so be patient; it may take time to correct the problems. It's important to be moving forward in the right direction.

DEALING WITH DECEIT

There is a difference between a communication disconnect and a total meltdown. When my computer has a system failure and I see the ugly blue screen, I first pray that the backup worked, and then I power down and restart. Sometimes it works; sometimes it doesn't, especially if I am dealing with a corrupted file or virus. With people, I can try to restart the conversation and rebuild a relationship, but if things are corrupted (anger, lying, deception and manipulation) then no matter what I try, without trust, the communication will stay superficial and cannot advance. You can't build a strong relationship on lies anymore than you can build a house on a mudslide.

Jesus had to deal with communication challenges and pressures that were extreme. When in public, he had to always be on his guard and never relax (hmm, sounds like the life of anyone in the public eye). But Jesus' pressure was more extreme. His life depended on it.

There were many groups who were looking for ways to trap him with questions. We only know of a few dozen examples, but no doubt Jesus dealt with hundreds if not thousands of aggressive questions. These questions were not the semi-polite press conference variety; they had all the intensity of cross-examination by an aggressive prosecuting attorney. To make it even worse, all of the different groups were doing "tag-team hand-offs."

The questions were difficult, but also potential traps. If Jesus answered in such a manner that was perceived as wrong or blasphemous, it could mean death. This is the intensity that we see in modern day demonstrations. For Jesus, the intensity was like a lynch mob. Several times they started to stone him, but failed. On his return to Bethany and Lazarus's grave, the disciples were hesitating about returning with him because of the death threats. But Thomas said to the others, *"Yes, we should go, so that we can die with him."* –John 11: 16, *Complete Jewish Bible.*

PREPARING FOR THE NASTY TRICK QUESTIONS – REFRAME, REBOUND AND SCORE!

Imagine your favorite basketball player who, in the final moments of a tied game, intercepts the ball on a rebound, drives down the court and at half court, swooshes the ball for a score as the clock runs out. Can you hear the roar of the crowd? Can you see the shocked and stunned looks on the faces of the opposing team? What the player did was reframe, rebound and score, which is a great way to deal with aggressive adversarial situations.

"Reframe, Rebound and Score" is the same sequence that Jesus demonstrated when he was attacked aggressively in public. These principles and techniques are well-proven strategies when dealing with crisis communication or media debates. When confronted by the Sadducees, Jesus refused to let the truth be taken down a level. He kept all the arguments in the court and wasn't swayed by the trick questions. See Luke 20: 27–39.

The question came from the Sadducees and was about the resurrection of the dead. They asked if a woman was a widow seven times over, then when she got to heaven, whose wife would she be? The trick part about this was that the Sadducees didn't believe in that there was life after death. They were asking Jesus what seemed to be a question to expand their faith, but which was in fact was a carefully laid net to trap him in one of the major theological arguments of his day. (Today, the question might be about the environment, abstinence or abortion.) Instead of giving them a Yes or No answer, Jesus countered by showing the foundational errors of the question.

Jesus reframed the argument and took the ball on the rebound. (He intercepted the question and shredded their argument. He explained that the focus on "whose wife would she be" did not matter in heaven because the rules are different.) Then, Jesus gave them true principles. (Resurrection changes everything. It's about heaven and eternity not the things of earth.) Jesus intercepted the question, returned to his side of the court and he shoots and scoooooooooooores! (He is God of the living, not dead.)

The results were that the experts were amazed. They told him that he gave a terrific answer, so good in fact that from that point on, no one dared to ask him anything. Talk about the ultimate shutout.

> *Crisis is opportunity riding on the dangerous wind.*
> – Dr. Edwin L. Cole

DEALING WITH DISASTERS

PONTIUS PILATE LESSONS FROM A MEDIA CRISIS

If someone ever had a media crisis, it was Pontius Pilate. It was a set-up from the start. Then it quickly spiraled into a major disaster. This was the ultimate no-win and became the most famous trial of all time. From the media crisis viewpoint, Pilate did almost everything right with the Jesus incident. Instead of focusing on the final score of this event, let's evaluate how the game was played. Frankly, Pilate's performance deserves reconsideration.

Looking at the way Pontius Pilate handled this situation, there are great take-away lessons. He used terrific PBI or "Pushback Implementation" in trying to avoid confrontation. Pilate used it all: sidestep, postpone, verify facts, hand-off, compromise, pacify and negotiate. He tried to keep Jesus from receiving the death penalty over and over in more than a dozen ways. He was courageous and insistent that Jesus was innocent. If Pilate performed by today's standards, his report card would show good grades for handling an impossible situation.

History has not been kind to Pilate. Josephus and others called him brutal, cruel and egotistic.[48] They said he took bribes. But all of these comments were written after his ten-year governorship in Palestine. For a few moments, let's consider the possibility of a different Pilate. Instead of the later, calloused politician, let's think of the young man in his thirties who had just gotten his first big assignment from the Emperor. What was this Pilate like when he arrived in Jerusalem? Was he intelligent, ambitious, energetic, proud, or culturally inexperienced? Did he have hopes and good intentions when he began?

WHO WAS PILATE?

Pontius Pilate's background is a matter of legend. One account contends that Pilate was the illegitimate son of a king. He was raised in Rome, exiled for murder to Asia Minor, where he gained success and was rewarded with the governorship of Judea. It is more likely that he was the son of Roman nobility and worked his way up the ladder of influence. The name Pilate means "Pike man" or one armed with a javelin.[49] Others translate it as "one who carries a spear." (That could be our equivalent of Lance or Spike.)

Pilate married very well. Claudia Procula was the granddaughter of Emperor Augustus and the illegitimate daughter of the third wife of the Emperor Tiberius. This may explain why Pilate got permission for his wife to come to the post.[50] What is curious is why she chose to leave the luxuries, relationships and privileges of Rome to accompany her husband to troubled areas like Judea and Jerusalem.

---

[48] *Josephus, The Works of Josephus*, Complete and Unabridged. Translated by William Whiston. Hendrickson Publishers, Peabody Mass. 1987, Book 18. Chapter 3.1–2 The Antiquities of the Jews Josephus.
[49] Page 350 *Who's Who in the Bible, The Old Testament and the Apocrypha, The New Testament*, by Joan Comay and Ronald Brownrigg, Wings Books, Random House Value Publishing, New York, NY, 1971.
[50] Page 351, *Who's Who*.

ROUGH BEGINNINGS – BUT THE EMPEROR APPROVED THE BUSINESS PLAN!

Imagine that you have finally gotten your first big assignment from Caesar who happens to be your wife's stepfather. Talk about pressure. Like many new executives, Pilate put together a strategic plan that they loved in Rome and the Boss approved, but the plan turned out to be a disaster in the field. Step One in Pilate's plan was to launch a PR campaign to reinforce the Roman authority and brand identity (through a billboard campaign with the Emperor's image in prominent locations). Jerusalem was the only city in the Empire whose citizens didn't bow to the emperor's statue in the city square. (The reason was that there wasn't a statute. Previous rulers made an exception due to fervent objections and Jewish beliefs.) Pilate was going to correct the oversight. Great concept in theory, but so wrong. (*But the consultants swore this plan worked in other cities.*)

His first week, Pilate marched into Jerusalem at night with soldiers carrying standards with images of the emperor on them. He then redecorated the area so everyone would notice. He hung the banners on walls facing the temple and then left town for his seaside home in Caesarea. Unfortunately, no one told him about the Graven Images memo. He didn't understand the pre-existing commitments from earlier rulers like his wife's grand-pappy Augustus, which excluded Jerusalem from the must-display-emperor's-mug rulings.

The next morning, Jerusalem was in an uproar. The chief priest Caiaphas shouted "Road trip!" Within 24 hours over 7,000 Jews streamed out of Jerusalem for a weeklong 24/7 prayer meeting in front of Pilate's house. When Pilate came to address them (with plans of killing enough to break up the crowd), they all said they would rather die than to accept graven images. In unity they knelt before the soldiers, offering their necks for execution.

Naturally, this passive display of rebellion unnerved and humiliated Pilate. He did not take military action. He had the Emperor's images taken down in Jerusalem and hung instead at his procuratorial residence. The rest of the story is that Caiaphas complained directly to Tiberius about the offensive banners, and Tiberius wrote to Pilate and told him to take them down. Score: Caiaphas 10, Pilate 0.

If at first you don't succeed....

Ok, so Pilate had a few bumps his first week in office, but there is nothing like a great public service project to make everyone love ya', right? Next, Pilate decided to give Jerusalem more water by building a new aqueduct. This was a great idea – fresh water, more jobs, more food, and more culture. Roman engineering was spectacular and had made desert areas like Pompeii into thriving communities. It was also a cultural improvement for who didn't love the public baths? Great concept but, once again, Pilate offended everyone. Instead of raising taxes, he took funds from the Temple treasury to pay for the building of the aqueduct. This is not a suggested way to win friends and build trusting relationships.

"However the Jews were not pleased with what had been done about this water; and many ten thousands of the people got together, and made a clamor against him, and insisted that he should leave off that design. Some of them also reproached, and abused the man, as crowds of such people usually do."[51] Josephus 18.3.2

Pilate was offended at the lack of appreciation for his civic improvements. It was time to teach a few lessons. Pilate took a few notes from the Godfather files and had his soldiers; dressed in plainclothes, go in to break up the throngs. Many of the protesters were slain and even more trampled to death in the temple area. To make it worse, some of those killed were Galileans and under Herod's rule. (Hey, nobody kills my guys, but me.)

THE JESUS INCIDENT

In the third year of his government, Pilate officiated over Jesus' trial. Pilate was in Jerusalem to keep order and monitor the Passover crowds. The normal population of Jerusalem was an estimated 100,000–200,000. More than 2.5 million Hebrews lived in

---

[51] *Josephus, The Works of Josephus*, Complete and Unabridged. Translated by William Whiston. Hendrickson Publishers, Peabody Mass, 1987, Book 18. Chapter 3.2 The Antiquities of the Jews.

the area,[52] but during the festivals the population swelled four to five times and more. Pilate only had about 3,000 troops and was restricted from calling in legions. With all the hatred toward Rome plus religious factions, crowds and visitors, it was an extremely stressful time.

During the festivals, Pilate and other Roman officials tried to keep a low profile, except for the regularly scheduled release of a prisoner. But when the religious leaders came knocking early in the morning, thus began one of the most difficult media and public challenges of Pilate's life.

THE TRIAL–PLAY BY PLAY

In reviewing the case from a crisis communication viewpoint, Pilate handled the situation extremely well. He used option after option, reason after reason, hour after hour, while struggling to avoid riots and more blood shed. It's interesting to see how many ways Pilate tried to dodge the bullet. It is interesting to note that the questions are grouped into four main areas. The four topics or areas break down into: details, facts, emotions and gut survival. These four areas should seem similar since they match the Multi-track technique from Chapter 7.

Pilate's pushback techniques can be used for dealing with adversarial situations or media crisis challenges.[53] Note that the following charts show that Pilate used twenty different arguments to avert disaster.

PILATE'S PUSBACK TECHNIQUE – A MEDIA CRISIS MODEL	
1) REMEMBER THE DETAILS	AVOID, SIDESTEP AND DODGE
Send the problem back from where it came.	Pilate said: *You be the judge.*
It's not my job.	Pilate said: *You have courts.*
It's not my expertise.	Pilate said: *Am I a religious judge? What is truth?*
It's not my expertise.	Pilate said: *It's Herod's job.*
Defer and stall and look for ways to pass situation to someone else quickly.	

---

[52] Page 320. *Mysteries of the Bible, The Enduring Questions of the Scriptures*, The Reader's Digest Association, Pleasantville, NY, 1988.
[53] The lists and charts of account of Pontius Pilate's experience with Jesus is based on all four gospels and *The Life of Jesus*, Tyndale House, Wheaton, IL, 2004. This book combines the gospels into a single enlightening narrative.

2) THINK YOUR WAY OUT Keep the dialogue going as long as possible.	USE THE FACTS FOR LEVERAGE ARGUE THE ISSUES ASK WHY?
No facts to support the claims.	Pilate asked: *What has he done?*
No basis for the charges.	Pilate asked: *Why do you bring him?*
No evidence or witness to substantiate.	Pilate: *Ask Jesus why?*
Defer and stall by asking for more information.	Pilate: *Questions Jesus*
3) APPEAL TO THE HEART	**ADDRESS THE EMOTIONS**
He's not guilty.	Pilate said: *I find him innocent*
Questions motives of crowd.	Pilate asked: *What do you want me to do?*
Asks crowd, *Do you really want the responsibility and guilt of condemning an innocent man to death?*	Pilate said: *I wash my hands of it.* After the crowd says, *Yes.*
4) GUT IT OUT WHEN THINGS ARE FALLING APART Pilate deals with mob as the last resort.	**REVERT TO SURVIVAL MODE** Ask questions on core issues Face the Public and keep your defenses up.
Compromise.	Pilate said: *I'll whip him instead of death.*
Negotiate.	Pilate asked: *Who shall I release Barrabas or Jesus?*
Renegotiate.	Pilate asked: *Who do you really want?*
Repeat.	Pilate said: *I'm not sure I heard correctly.*
Refuse.	Pilate said: *Do what you believe is best.*

SITUATION	PUSH BACK	PILATE RESPONSES
Jesus presented for death penalty. Council claims disturbing peace, tax evasion and claims to be King of the Jews.	1. Not my job!	Pilate refuses: "Take care of it yourself." You have your own court, guards and have stoning. I thought you had to wait 24 hours before death penalty? What's the rush?
Jesus questioned about King thing; Jesus says "You say I am."	2. No case.	Pilate dismisses on grounds of religious not political issue, technicality. Asks Jesus: Are you King of Jews? What have you done to upset them?
Jesus: "I came to bring truth into the world."	3. No facts.	Pilate says, "What is Truth?" Not seeing much here. Pilate asks for facts and support of charges so he can dismiss the case. (C'mon Jesus, give me something to work with here!)
Council accuses Jesus of riots in Galilee and Jerusalem.	4. Not my Jurisdiction.	Pilate defers and passes the buck to Herod for ruling – Jesus is from his 'hood. Let Herod deal with the Jewish leaders. (This is the escape clause I was looking for.)
Herod wants a miracle. Jesus says nothing, while Hebrew leaders keep accusing.	5. No basis for charges.	Herod questions Jesus and even with no response decides he is innocent. Knows that this is a no win. Takes a pass on making an unpleasant ruling before the long holiday weekend. Uses opportunity to dig at the religious leaders by mocking Jesus as King and giving him a royal robe. Sends him back to Pilates' docket.

SITUATION	PUSH BACK	PILATE RESPONSES
Jesus returns with new outfit. Council takes time to stir up crowd.	6. Not guilty.	Pilate says Herod and I agree, he's innocent. Uses weight of joint effort to shutdown proceedings.
Crowd surges forward demanding the Passover prisoner be released.	7. Stalls.	Pilate measures and listens to the crowd. Pilate's wife sends note– Dream analysis says Jesus is good guy, leave him alone.
Crowd continues demands of death penalty for Jesus.	8. Offers compromise.	Pilate has Jesus whipped to teach him a lesson and satisfy the charges of civil disobedience.
Crowd gets uglier, crying out for blood.	9. Appeals to mob and shows them a bloody Jesus.	Pilate tries to satisfy bloodlust and offer compassion: "Here is your King."
Crowd cries.	10. Not guilty.	What do you want me to do with him? I find him innocent!
Crowd asks to crucify him.	11. Negotiates.	Pilate offers limited choice of Barrabas or Jesus for release.
Crowd chooses Barrabas.	12. You're responsible.	Pilate asks: What do YOU want me to do with Jesus? Are you sure about this?
Crowd says kill him!	13. Refuses request.	Pilate just says no. Won't do it. I say he is innocent, you do it.
Leaders expose motivation– they want Jesus put to death for claiming to be Son of God.	14. Seeks truth from the source.	Pilate shaken by Jesus claiming to be the Son of God. Asks Jesus, "Who are you really? Where do you come from?" Please give me a reason to help you.
Jesus says your power comes from my Father.	15. Tries to release Jesus.	Pilate afraid. Wife may be right.

SITUATION	PUSH BACK	PILATE RESPONSES
Jewish leaders: "He's an enemy of Rome, we demand you crucify him. We'll tell if you don't."	16. Pilate trapped. No way out but back to the mob.	Pilate knows this is a threat to notify Caesar that he didn't take action against a person who was considered dangerous and a threat to peace and stability. Chief Priest Caiaphas had created problems with Emperor already. (Seven years later Caiaphas got Pilate ousted.)
Crowd yells, Barrabas wins the vote.	17. Negotiates.	Pilate offers–who do you want me to release? Jesus or Barrabas. He reminds them again that Jesus is innocent.
Crowd yells again.	18. Asks again.	Pilate asks again. Are you Sure?
Crowd replies the same.	19. Asks again.	Pilate repeats question. Are there any other ballots?
Crowd grows louder and takes responsibility for crucifixion.	20. Passes responsibility.	Pilate hands off the decision, accepts the answer of the mob. Pushes back blame on them.
Crowd accepts blame.	21. Washes hands– symbolic act.	Pilate washes his hands in front of the mob to symbolize his innocence and stepping away from the sentence.
Jesus taken for execution.	22. Case closed, but posts sign.	Pilate releases the order for the crucifixion. Writes sign, Jesus of Nazareth, King of the Jews in three languages.
Jewish leaders protest the sign.	23. Sign stays!	Pilate has had it. Was the sign intentional or by accident? Who knows but Pilate was on his last nerve and told them to forget it, sign stays, get outta' here!

PILATE HAS THE FINAL WORD

Jesus was accused of causing riots, not paying taxes and calling himself the King of the Jews. None of these charges motivated Pilate to crucify Jesus. During his trial, when the Jewish leaders found no success, they pushed harder. They accused Jesus of being an enemy of Rome. They claimed to be law-abiding citizens who were doing their duty to bring this matter to the attention of Rome. If Pilate did not take action against Jesus, then he was not a friend to Caesar. This was the trump card that pushed Pilate into the judgment seat.

From this account, Pilate used twenty different pushback techniques to avoid disaster. For a thirty-year old governor with riot conditions, he did exceptionally well. He appealed with multi-track questions, returned to facts, negotiated and renegotiated. Pilate had been set up and caught in a web of deception and manipulation. Like a man wrestling against a straightjacket, he tried every way to get out of crucifying Jesus. When he ran out of options, he stepped back from the table, released the decision, passed the buck, and let the religious elite have their way. During the process, his own wall began to crumble when Jesus claimed to be the Son of God. It says he was more afraid then ever. Pilate went and asked Jesus, "Where are you from?"

Even though his hand was forced, Pilate had the final slam against the Jewish leaders. On the wooden cross, he had a sign nailed above Jesus' head, that read, ***Jesus the Nazarene the King of the Jews*** in Hebrew, in Latin and in Greek. This was the major claim that the religious council brought against Jesus. How furious they must have been to see the sign. According to John's Gospel, the chief priests protested and Pilate told them to take a hike and leave it alone. He threw the charges back in their face. He said that *what he had written was written.*

APPLICATION

Have you ever had a situation where you did every thing right and no matter what you did, the end result was a disaster? It doesn't seem fair when things like that happen. It is easy to take offense. As we learn, we see life isn't fair, it just "is." It is what we do with what "is" that makes the difference. Life is a struggle and the earth is a battlefield. Some battlegrounds are external horrid conditions and others are internal twisted shadows. Even the privileged become prodigals and have a struggle. At the base level, faith knows that we aren't alone in this struggle. We will overcome on some level, whatever happens.

When you find yourself in difficult communication situations, there are some basic tools that you can use. When you have a problem with an individual, use the term communication disconnect instead of breakdown to address the issues. When encountering deceitful situations, use the facts and use logic to unseat the arguments. The questions are not the issue. People's hearts are. For media crisis situations that appear to be disastrous, use pushback implementation to avoid the situation. In a set-up situation, you don't want to play. Get off the field as soon as possible, as fast as possible.

DEALING WITH NO-WINS AND DEATH

WHEN JESUS DID NOT SPEAK

It was a perfect spring morning on the east coast. I was writing with the windows open enjoying the breeze and gentle beauty of the woods around my friend Anne's house. A spontaneous stream of birdsong floated in through the window.

Like a well-rehearsed choir they flowed from chorus to solo to aria for hours. Dozens of golden finches were flashing through the dogwoods with chirrups. Chickadees joined in to provide a staccato accent after the robin's alto solo. Not to be forgotten, the cardinals called with a second soprano cry that was sustained like a diva wanna-be. The jays sounded out like an army bugle. The downy woodpeckers gave an intermittent tapping that provided a bold rhythm. I breathed deeply enjoying the unique symphony of bird song that was never to be repeated.

Then suddenly things were quiet. As if someone pushed the pause button. Nothing. Without the benefit of electronic switch, signal light or warning system, over a hundred birds had gone into silence. As I wondered what had happened, there was a screech from far above the treetops. A hawk had entered the area and all the songbirds became silent and motionless, waiting for the hawk leave the area.

Several minutes passed and after a final lazy circle, the hawk glided west toward the river. Slowly the birds began to sing again. One tweet, one chirp, then two notes and followed by a currup. The birds knew instinctively when to be silent because their life depended on it. And knew when it was safe to sing again.

If birds can know when to be silent then shouldn't we? In a noisy world it is hard to embrace silence. The rule with commercials is just turn up the amps, increase the orchestration, bring on the dancers, add some flash, spinning graphics and lights. Silence is usually the last option because silence may mean that we spend some time thinking.

JESUS SAID NOTHING

Jesus was a brilliant communicator but he also knew *the oft-forgotten secret*, the key to communication power, which is when to not speak. In a word saturated world, this lesson is counter intuitive and difficult. We want to defend ourselves and justify our actions. It takes wisdom to speak but discernment guides us when words are pointless.

There are many times that Jesus did not respond and answer the questions that were thrown at him. As explained previously he did not answer the challenges of those who simply wanted to argue or use him to make themselves look better. Jesus didn't waste time with verbal sparring. He refused to get into the ring and often publicly called them on their motives.

DID HE DIE WELL?

In the movie, *Lady Jane* after the execution of a noble, the question is asked, "Did he die well?" This movie tells the story of Lady Jane Grey who was made Queen of England after the death of Edward, son of Henry VIII. After nine days on the throne, Mary and the Catholic supporters overthrow her. Even though she was a teen, she and her husband were beheaded.

Those who were not at the execution wanted to know what happened. Did they face death like a noble? Did they keep their faith? What did they say? Did they die well?[54]

Unless a seed dies....

I assure you: Unless a grain of wheat falls into the ground and dies, it remains by itself. But if it dies, it produces a large crop and the one who loves his life will lose it, and the one who hates his life in this world will keep it for eternal life. – Jesus, John 12: 24–25, *HCSB*

Jesus knew who he was and what his mission was so he did not panic in the face of death. He battled through his doubts and fears in the Garden of Gethsemane the previous night. He had spoken to his soul; he had strengthened his spirit, focused his resolve and calmed himself. The worst was coming but he was prepared and it did not change his mission. He had accepted the cup that was given to him and drank it fully.

In less than eighteen hours he was brought before five different courts without an attorney, witness or deposition. Yet, question after question and accusation after accusation, he refused to speak. Though he could have crushed their arguments or preformed a miracle to silence them, he resisted the natural desire for the eternal goal.

His silence frustrated Pilate, *"Don't you know that I have the power to set you free?"*

Jesus responded, *"The only power that you have is what My Father has given to you."* Even when faced with the possibility of a

---

54 *Lady Jane*, Paramount Pictures, 1986; starring Helena Bonham Carter, Cary Elwes, Patrick Stewart, Directed by Trevor Nunn.

worldly escape hatch, Jesus reminded Pilate that he, too, was a player on an eternal stage.

By not speaking, Jesus reset the argument and changed the lens. Trials that were meant to be an indictment turned and convicted those that brought the charges. On this dreadful day, Jesus did not speak and the world was blessed forever.

Unless a seed dies, it will not live to its purpose.

CHAPTER 11
QUANTUM COMMUNICATION

When once you have tasted flight, you will forever walk the earth with your eyes turned skyward, for there you have been, and there you will always long to return.
– Leonardo Da Vinci

IT'S ALL ABOUT COMMUNICATION

Communication is the essence of life. It is the glue that builds relationships and the force that makes the stars hold hands. From the stars to the atoms, communication is everlasting. Sometimes we can see it. Sometimes we hear it, but often we just feel it. The planets dance around the sun in their orbits. Electrons whirl around neutrons. Their dance explodes into spectrums of light and beauty that we perceive with the human eye. Where does the music come from that guides this dance? We can see the waltz and join in as we watch the stars domed across the sky.

DANCE OF THE STARS

They say we can hear the stars singing. I wonder if the stars dance to their own tune, or does their dance birth a new song that follows their trajectory like a prancing child? From stars to our hearts, from atoms to the billions of electrons in the brain, we depend on communication to exist. The base element of communication is a harmony that we need to live. When we are filled with gladness, we can feel our bodies tremble with joy. When we are devastated with grief we shiver as hope drains out of us.

ARE THERE SOUND PARTICLES?

Light and sound both travel on waves that we can hear and feel. Whether it is a speaker with a microphone or a gentle song, even if we can't feel them our ears and bodies respond to the vibrations. The last and most controversial of Einstein's theories was that light was both energy and had mass. Einstein believed that light contained tiny particles of mass that impacted the objects they touched or passed through. Sir Isaac Newton first proposed that light consisted of tiny particles when he discovered that white light when it passes through a prism separates into a rainbow. When energy emissions can be measured it is said to be quantized.

Einstein discovered that light comes in tiny packets of energy known as quanta, which explains how light behaves as a particle in certain experiments and a wave in others. These particles of light are called photons. This theory is being studied, but when we consider the impact of a laser, which is concentrated light, Einstein was probably correct. Light may be both energy and mass.

And if light and sound both travel on waves then might not the same principal apply to sound? Sound can be quantized, measured and manipulated. We use sonic technology to heal and to navigate, but could sound be composed of tiny particles that are carried in the sound waves. If so, could then our words act like the quanta packets for light, to help them release different values of energy?

How can we explain why plants, animals and our bodies respond to positive words? Scientists took subatomic pictures of water before and after positive versus negative words were spoken over it. Positive words like love and prayer resulted in the water molecules being formed in lovely balanced crystalline formations like snowflakes. When negative and hateful words were spoken over the water, the molecules became jagged and misaligned. If speaking positive words can change basic water, how will positive words change a human being who is 75% water? Is this one of the reasons prayer works?

Words are more than simple sounds. They are a force. Life and death are in the power of our words. And all of us have experienced the positive and the negative effects of words. How do we quantize our words? Could it be that our words are more than sound, but have a physical and spiritual impact on others as well?

GIVE ME THE MOON

In the classic fable, *Many Moons* by James Thurber, in a land far away a princess has become sickly. The King asks why. She tells him that she will only be well if she has the moon in the sky. The King challenges all the wise men in the kingdom to find a way to capture the moon for his precious daughter. All efforts fail until finally the court jester asks the princess what size the moon was. And in the simple clarity of a child, she tells him that the moon is only as large as her thumbnail and could be held in her hand. The king makes a silver moon for his daughter to wear and all is well in the kingdom.[55]

Great communicators know how to put the moon in our hands. Jesus put more than the moon in people's hands. He gave them a ladder to reach the moon, and the stars and eternity. He gave them a road to their hearts, each other and truth. Jesus connected them to the universe, both above and within. Through his words, Jesus was able to communicate complex issues and make it look so easy.

JESUS AS THE MASTER COMMUNICATOR

Jesus used words in a powerful way. He spoke with love and simplicity.

Jesus taught the true spirit of communication, because he knew that true communication comes from the spirit.

Maybe it is all about connecting. Atom to Adam. Heart to Hope. Spirit to Light. Communication is the way that we connect. Jesus came and taught people how to connect and reconnect. He

[55] Thurber, James, *Many Moons*, 1943.

taught them to connect with each other, themselves and the Father. He used simple words to help take people from the dusty roads of life into the gardens of heaven. He walked and lived fully.

As we transition into this new Information Age, this renaissance made possible by man's mastery of electronics, we must not forget what guided our past. In a world of excessive information it may become easy to forget to connect. We must not substitute virtual connection for that which is real, genuine and life-giving. The intercourse of our lives creates a rich complex orchestration. No amount of electronic interaction will ever create a child. We must touch. We must kiss. We must embrace. We must communicate.

We must remember that WE must change the map of our communications orientation. We must remember that OUR words are the source of real life and the electricity of community.

Your hands may never draw a masterpiece.

Your work may never make a fortune.

Your thoughts may never create a company.

Your actions may never craft a monument.

But your words can do this and so much more.

Words can create.

Words can refresh.

Words can inspire the new and the old.

Words can teach the ignorant and the wise.

Words can touch a face or eternity.

Words can be remembrance or encumbrance.

Words give life, joy, peace, courage, strength...just speak.

All of us have words. Everyday, everywhere.

Millions and millions of words are waiting....

Like the dew waiting to nourish the fields and flowers,

Like fruit and leaves for the healing of nations,

Like fallen manna to feed those in the desert,

We just have to gather them.

Will you get your baskets?

Will you plant wisely?

Will you speak light?

There is birth, love, laughter, hope, just breathe...and speak.

AUTHOR OVERVIEW

Lynn Scarborough's diverse media experience demonstrates how many opportunities are available to those with flexible communication skills. Ms. Scarborough's career includes: Broadcast Consultant for Television News, Media Trainer, Public Relations, Producer, Writer, Speaker and Teacher.

The author is President of EmPowercom, a firm specializing in media training and public relations for news organizations, corporations, not-for-profits and faith-based organizations. Over the past twenty years, the author has worked with over two hundred news operations including CBS, ABC, CNN and FOX. Since 1980, she has conducted over six thousand individual coaching sessions with television journalists, athletes and business leaders across the continent. Clients have included: Paula Zahn, Catherine Crier, Debbie Norville, Isaiah Thomas, Hannah Storm, Forest Sawyer, Sarah James, Carol Linn, Tony Dorsett.

Ms. Scarborough has provided corporate communications training and media coaching for clients such as Capital One Auto Finance, G.S.A., Silicon Graphics, Chrysler, National Organization of Women Legislators (NOWL), Kellogg Foundation, Global Celebration for Women and Covenant Training Institute. She developed the Strategic Business Communication Training™ and Communication Bootcamp™, which are designed to increase productivity in the Information Technology and Agile environments.

Ms. Scarborough has provided public relations and writing services for clients including MannaTech, The Brainy Baby Company, Breakthroughs in Health, Manna Relief Ministries, Laub

BioChem Inc., and ministries such as Christian Men's Network and Youth for Christ.

Production credits include: Manna Relief Ministries, Somebody Cares Documentary, The Call (D.C.), Global Pastors Wives Network and Executive Producer for the Senate Congressional Office for the Re-dedication of the Suffragettes Statue (broadcast on C-SPAN).

Ms. Scarborough is a Life Coach and author of *Spiritual Moms, An Inspirational Guide for Women of Influence*, which teaches others how to mentor others through all the seasons of life. In the humanitarian arena Ms. Scarborough has been writing and working with a wide range of issues including AIDS orphans, sex trafficking, and nutrition. When she is not traveling, Lynn makes her home in North Texas and enjoys photography, gardening and playing softball.

AUTHOR NOTES
Funny Thing Happened on the Way to My Destiny, I had the Wrong Map!

A funny thing happened on my way to my destiny, I had the wrong map. Come to think of it, I didn't even have the right universe much less the correct instruction book. As a college student, how can you plan for a career and a job description that hasn't been written? Like many before me, even the best of planning, dreaming and goal setting through high school, college and graduate school days never gave me a glimpse of where life and the long and winding road would take me.

Like many 20-somethings, after years of college, I was on the quest to find the "One Perfect Career." The continual (and reasonable) questions from concerned parents and well meaning relatives all had one common thread: "What are you going to dooooooooooooooooo with your life?"

After several degrees and multiple universities, my unspoken response to those questions was "Frankly, Daddy, I don't have a clue." All I had was inclinations, hopes, dreams, goals and prayer. Like most twenty-year-olds, I didn't know that the "One Perfect Career" was a cultural myth. I was looking for the "One Thing" and missed the map. I thought that building a career was like choosing the right airplane ticket, but, in fact, it was more like jumping off a cliff into a rain swollen river and grabbing hold of something that would help you make it through the rapids.

Most people never end up doing what they thought they wanted to do when they graduated. More importantly, most people have multiple careers that build into futures that look totally different than their youthful life plans. What I naïvely thought would play out like a clean business flow chart or a working Caribbean cruise was more like a Willy Wonka freefall. That is an exciting part of the career journey and, like childbirth and building a house, once the pain is forgotten, it can later be romanticized.

Before arriving at the threshold of electronic media, I collected a variety of degrees from several colleges with the objective of being a theater professor and an expert in Children's Theatre and Creative Dramatics. In the theater department, I learned how to help actors transform themselves into lively characters and transform the words of a play into a living experience that transported the audience into other times and worlds. As a creative dramatics teacher, I led children, teachers, the elderly and those with special needs into a time of joyful play, self-discovery and healing through communal activities. During graduate school I took courses in England and at an Episcopal Seminary to expand my personal and spiritual vistas, though not necessarily in that order of importance.

After leaving the security of graduate school at the University of Texas, I took a job as the Dean of the Casa Mañana Theatre school in Ft. Worth which led to a job producing local children's television programs in Dallas, which led to what I believed would be a short-term job with a Dallas-based Television News Consulting firm. These jobs were separated by months of pounding the pavements in Dallas, NYC and LA to find jobs in acting, modeling or production assistant work. I had to take the short-term job as a consultant to have medical insurance because I had developed vocal nodules from incorrect training from acting teachers. The job with the news consulting firm would help tide me over until I raised enough money to move to Los Angeles and work toward the big break into the entertainment industry.

Without realizing it, my education and early career days flowed together to prepare me for a remarkable journey. Looking back, it is amazing how even the "boring graduate classes" and what seemed to be unimportant meetings helped to guide me into a stream that led to a great river of opportunities. Like a Lewis and Clark expedition, my career path launched into the uncharted territory of television journalism during the eighties. What I didn't realize until later was that the consulting job that I took out of desperation was really my big break.

The company that I was working for was one of less than a handful of independent consultant groups that helped stations in cities both large and small to launch and develop their newscasts into the profitable morning, noon, and evening timeslots. My job was to help find, hire and develop the "talent" or on-camera anchors, reporters, sportscasters and weathercasters for local television stations. When we first started the coaching division, most news people would come into Dallas for training, but soon I was bouncing from newsroom to newsroom across the country.

After starting my own company, I averaged over 170 days a year on the road for fifteen years. I stopped counting after 6,000 coaching sessions with over 200 newsrooms in every major city in America. Everyone has to begin somewhere and I helped develop people like Paula Zahn, Deborah Norville, Forest Sawyer, Sarah James, Catherine Crier and sports figures like Tony Dorsett, Isaiah Thomas, Dan Jiggetts, plus dozens of politicians, CEO and authors.

WHAT IS A MEDIA COACH?

When I began media coaching, most people didn't understand what I did. Regardless of the field – sports, sales, acting, life or media – a coach helps people to be their best in every situation. But just as professional athletes depend on coaches to maximize their performance, people need direction and feedback to help them maximize their presentation when in front of the camera. I helped people improve their presentation skills when on television news or in any media situation. Clients included corporate executives dealing with a media crisis to the professional journalist for national networks or local television stations. Regardless of the size of the market, everyone needs constructive feedback to help improve.

We have all watched and critiqued the network anchors, politicians and celebrities. We compare the performance of our local weather guy to that of the network big wigs and criticize them when they don't meet our expectations. Unfortunately, although unfair, this reality makes being on television today more difficult than twenty years ago. The challenge that most people deal with when in front of the camera is that the rules for effective communication are different than when in a one-on-one situation.

In the 80's, the local television news industry started to explode. The growth of lower cost video technology and increased advertising revenues contributed to the massive growth. Stations that only had one 6 o'clock newscast were adding news at noon, 5:00, 5:30, 10:00, 11:00, and more. The news departments were doubling and tripling in size, making it difficult to find qualified people (especially women and minorities) to fill the on-camera and off air positions. It was a great time to try to get an on-camera news job. What a change from today, when even the beginning reporter position for a job in a small city like Reno or Birmingham garners hundreds of audition tapes with over 90% of the applications being female.

During the 80's, those of us in the news media never knew the expanse of the territory that was in front of us. We worked so hard and fast that we never had time to fully realize that we were pioneers exploring and building the infrastructure of local news departments for communities across the nation. It was like building the space shuttle once you were already in orbit. It was exciting and addictive to jump on airplanes, whoosh into newsrooms, research the mindset of a new community, network with smart and attractive people, problem solve public relations issues, coach people to new levels of achievement, and dodge the arrows of resentment that came from those who wanted to maintain the status quo in the ratings.

We had the opportunity to be in newsrooms and watch hundreds of remarkable and historic events unfold. When a news story hits, the feeling is electric. It's similar to a wartime MASH unit as dozens of people begin a frenzy of information gathering, phones ringing, scanners screeching, printers buzzing – like bees streaming out of a shaken hive, executives rush to man the battle stations alongside the interns to capture and process information. Crisis calls forth the best from a newsroom. You can watch television and films about newsrooms or hospital emergency rooms, but there is nothing like being in the middle of news events as a team of people try to gather information, shaping and then catapulting it out into the airwaves. For those who are made to handle the pressure (or are addicted to the crisis), it is a terrific career.

The 80's and the mid-90's produced some great journalism and established a standard that the rest of the world had yet to follow. It was a time of birthing, vision, excitement and exhaustion. This was the time before the impact of deregulation and before the industry was sold out to the Wall Street demagoguery. This was a time when local managers had to answer to their friends and to their daily business contacts as to the content of their newscast. This was a time when journalists were respected and admired. It was a time when there was accountability and often serious consequences for actions. It was a time before the quality of journalism was sacrificed on the altar of consumerism and television stations were flipped faster than pancakes at IHOP. I don't mean to preach, but I did learn something at seminary.

It was my experience in the Television News industry, that among the overwhelming majority of us who call ourselves journalists (whether on-air, management or consultants), there was an unwritten creed of focus, truth and integrity. People got fired for lying and inappropriate endorsement of political parties or agendas. We knew that journalism was the last voice for the little guys. We held our responsibility as sacred and a matter of life, death, truth and justice for the communities that we served. For many true journalists there is a visionary mindset and warrior heart that is driven by truth and a desire to help others. To be a true journalist requires a tremendous amount of dedication, sacrifice and courage. Those who are serving in war zones and in foreign countries with oppressive governments know the huge and often horrible cost that is required for the by-line.

On a side note, I am weary of all the media bashing from all corners of the world. There needs to be some balance and respect for the sacrifice, contributions, and value that our media has provided. To say that all media purveyors are bad is like putting on a victimized poverty mindset and lumping all politicians, attorneys, preachers, insurance salesmen and doctors into the crooked-greedy-lose-'em-all bucket. Even as flawed as our media system is, it still is the best in the world and in the history of mankind. It has great power to protect, inform, educate and entertain.

In many situations and communities, the News Industry in all its forms – newspapers, radio, television and Internet – is the only and last defender of the "little guy." Thank God for our freedom of the press which, even though tested continually within our borders, protects our journalists and publishers from assassination and imprisonment. (For the first time in the history of war, terrorists are using journalists as pawns in their negotiations.) Think of all that we expect and have come to depend upon from media journalists: up to the second information on news, finances, sports, weather, consumer goods, in addition to investigative work that protects us from criminals, corporate greed, government misconduct, sexual predators, natural disasters and more. In our world, every day our lives are protected, saved and valued by the many media voices. The challenge in our now media saturated and media cynical world is getting the information to those who need it most.

But let me return to my journey through journalism. The end of the nineties marked a change in the news business for many independent consultants and journalists. For about ten years, corporations had been buying and selling stations like baseball cards and the control of the local television stations and news decisions shifted to corporate entities that dealt with a small number of consulting companies to tell them what to do. Some were good, but several of the larger ones had been transformed into marketing machines that dispensed facts, tricks and tools.

Deregulation affected America's journalism, for better and for worse, and like other industries journalism was forever changed by vertical integration, supply chain economics, political dancing and Wall Street waltzing. The smaller and mid-size media companies were swept into stock offerings created by faceless CPA firms. When the profit margins of stations shrunk, then the consolidation and cuts for personnel, programs, and news services were made at the local level. People complain that the news looks the same, but without resources and personnel, local stations don't have the luxury of diversity. Add to this the economic hardship of 9/11. When a war or major news event happens, like other industries, television budgets immediately shift into survival mode. Like a dog shaking off the rain, many of my fellow consultants and journalists were thrown back into the job market to morph into new careers.

Not being able to compete with the financial tactics of the large consulting firms and being tired of years on the road, I decided to work on the other side of the camera in public relations. Being one for causes, I worked with groups that dealt with social, political and health issues, such as sex slavery, AIDS orphans and urban social reform. I helped companies and individuals get their messages into the mainstream media by training them with the same techniques that professional journalists use and by helping shape their message like a television producer.

Regardless of the industry, consulting and coaching requires an ever-expanding combination of tools, skills and understanding. As with any teacher, the needs and response of the students affect your performance. The greater the desire, the better the exchange.

Working with non-profits and ministries helped me discover the great need and desire for media exposure, as well as the even greater fear people had of being in front of the camera and interacting with the media. Hence, the development of several curricula that would help people become "Fearless Communicators"™ in any presentation situation, from television to public speaking. For corporations, we developed the "Strategic Business Communication Training" to help them maximize their management, improve teamwork and deal with daily communication disconnects.

HOW DID *TALK LIKE JESUS* EVOLVE?

Experience teaches us that there is nothing new under the sun – but there is always a new story about it on the 10:00 news. If we are honest with ourselves, truth will keep us humble and change will help us grow.

Over the last six years, the sessions with more faith-based groups helped me realize how many of the modern communication techniques were used by Jesus of Nazareth. As I began to strip away previous concepts, it was as if all the sevens clicked into line and the mental jackpot clanged like a fire engine. I love those moments of great revelation in which you discover the most obvious of truths was right in front of you, like, when the car keys are shoved under a paper on your desk.

In a recent newspaper interview, a reporter asked me if I used Jesus as a model when working with mainstream networks. In truth, I probably did; it was subconscious. During my sessions (and in Chapter 4), the foundational questions are, "What is a Master Communicator?" During the discussion of the techniques and role models, clients often referenced Jesus along with other role models. Personally, I have always admired, studied and learned from Jesus' examples both as a student and as a teacher in Sunday school, youth groups and adult education.

Sometimes in life it isn't a matter of having all the answers, but wisdom comes when we take the time to rethink the questions. So with my frenetic newsroom days behind me, I began to look more deeply and simply at the nature of communication in our hyper-media world. One principle lead to another and another and then, suddenly, all the communication theory, exercises and stories mentally morphed into a different image. Like clothes shrunk by the drier, there was no going back. So it was time to revamp and after several years, this book is the first harvest of what has been, and is being, discovered.

One of the major things that I have discovered is how much this understanding has changed my own communication style across the board. Others who have begun integrating these techniques have reported new success in their daily interaction at the office, home, community and ministry and with family, spouses, children, friends, employees, bosses and advisors.

I'VE BEEN IN "REWRITE"

Before writing my first book, I attended writer's conferences and listened to other authors explain that sometimes books came from within. Sometimes a book dropped on an author and changed them. When I started this book, it was never expected that learning and studying Jesus' communication methods and techniques would cause such a "rewrite" of my life. Words, thoughts, decisions and actions, the entire cycle is being transformed. Learning to *Talk Like Jesus* has made a difference in my life and the lives of others. As I shared earlier, my objective is to empower you with tools and encourage you to become a more successful communicator. Thank you for joining me and giving me an opportunity to share the S.I.M.P.L.E.™ Method of my Master Communicator and the lover of my soul.

May your spirit have life and your words be light!

ACKNOWLEDGMENTS

While I thought that I was learning how to live, I have been learning how to die.
— Leonardo Da Vinci

A seed dies so a plant can be born. Creative expression follows the same principle. This book has been a splendid birth, which was preceded by an extraordinary and lengthy process of death. There are many who can share in the joy of this harvest.

First credit goes to Diane Nine, my visionary agent, for recognizing the value of this project. Many thanks, Diane, for your amazing network, and for the tireless efforts that you and Clare extended to find the right home for this book.

For help with the pruning, my deepest appreciation to Janna Hughes for editing and listening to the spirit of the book. Thanks for the laughter and the long hours.

To my many clients and students, thanks for teaching me so much.

For support through difficult seasons, many thanks to Karen and Bill Callihan – without your love and generosity this would have never happened. To my many soul sisters – Karen S., Jackie, Michelle, Joanne, Carol and dozens of others; thanks for the friendship and prayers. Thanks, Jerry and Bill, for computer help at critical stages. Thanks to Chris, Cory, Heidi and Addi for graphics, editing and lattes.

For the refreshing hospitality, thanks to Annie Barge, Lucille Walker, Cris Campbell, Nancy Huston Hansen, Pearl Crisler, Bob and Barbara Prim, Rajean and Gary Vawter. Dearest Annie Barge, how can I thank you and Bev for the many years of love and friendship? Annie, I deeply appreciate the glorious spring in Virginia and your servant heart that helped this book evolve beyond the embryonic stages. To the late Rev. Bev Barge, thanks for being a great spiritual dad. I hope that some of your writing genius was transferred while using your books for research. It felt good to have you looking over my shoulder.

For the plowing into my life I am grateful for all the dear friends, councilors, and godly elders in my life. Thanks to a great community with Shady Grove Church in Grand Prairie, Texas (a grand place whose prairie days are long gone). To a wonderful community of friends, family and saints, my heartfelt thanks.

Finally, to my family – you know my heart and affection. Thanks for the support through the ups and downs. To Mom, Dad, Fell, Catherine, Burke, and sweet Annie – love always.

Just like the flowerpot cannot take credit for the beauty of the flower that is placed within it, so I cannot take credit for the revelations found here. The true credit goes to the seed. I have been privileged to be the container and provide the soil and the abundant fertilizer of experiences. The Father made the seed, Jesus is the light, the Holy Spirit gives the water and I have been the simple soil. And, yet the seed grows. Oh faithful wonders and glorious mysteries! Lord, let Thy will be in done in this earth as it is in Heaven.

Summary Information on Bibles Used

BIBLES USED IN TALK LIKE JESUS

1. *THE MESSAGE*, **The New Testament**, Eugene H. Peterson, NavPress, Colorado Springs, CO, 1993.
2. *Holy Bible, Holman Christian Standard Bible (HCSB)*, Holman Bible Publishers, Nashville, TN, 2004.
3. *Archaeological Study Bible, New International Version (NIV)*, Zondervan, Grand Rapids, MI, 2005.
4. *Complete Jewish Bible*, Translation by David H. Stern, Jewish New Testament Publications, Clarksville, MD, 1998.
5. *Life Application Study Bible, New International Version (NIV)*, Published by Tyndale House Publishers, Inc, Wheaton IL, and Zondervan Publishing House, Grand Rapids, MI, co 1988, 1989, 1990, 1991.
6. *The Life of Jesus*, Tyndale House, Wheaton, IL, 2004.
7. *The Layman's Parallel New Testament*, Zondervan Publishing House, Grand Rapids, MI, 1970.
   Comparing four popular translations–*The King James Version, The Amplified New Testament, The Living New Testament. The Revised Standard Version*
8. *The Amplified New Testament*, co. 1958, The Lockman Foundation, La Habra, CA.
9. *The Living New Testament*, co. 1967, Tyndale House Foundation, Wheaton, IL.
10. *Revised Standard Version*, co. 1946, 1952, by Division of Christian Education, of the National Council of Churches of

Christ, in the United States of America. The test for the Revised Standard Version of the New Testament is used by permission of the Division of Christian Education, National Council of Churches, Zondervan Publishing House, Licensee. First printing August 1970, second printing September 1970, Third printing December 1970.

11. *The Four Translation New Testament*, Printed for Decision Magazine by Worldwide Publications, Minneapolis, MN, 1966.

These are the four versions contained within it. King James Version, New American Standard, Williams, New Testament in the Language of the People and Beck, New Testament in the Language of Today.

12. *Williams, New Testament in the Language of the People,*
Charles B. Williams, Moody Press, 1963.

13. *Beck, New Testament in the Language of Today,*
William F. Beck, Concordia Publishing House, St. Louis, MO, 1963; Concordia Publishing Ltd, London WC, 1963.